JAN 98

A SOUTH AFRICAN GUIDE TO HERBS

A SOUTH AFRICAN GUIDE TO
HERBS
BARBARA HEY

STRUIK

Author's Acknowledgements

The author would like to thank the following people:
Andrew Russell of 'Turtle Rock' for Companion Planting with
Herbs (page 13) and for his advice and support;
Pat Nicholson for the recipe for Jeyes Fluid Spray (page 14);
Dave Golding for the recipe for Red Pepper Spray (page 14);
John Simpson, well-known garden adviser, for his invaluable tip on
compost activators (page 9);
Anthony Johnson (photographer) and Vo Pollard (stylist) for the
photographs on pages 16, 18 and 22;
Marguerite Fischer, Jackie Ravenscroft and the Cape Town
Herb Group for their friendly assistance.

Struik Publishers (Pty) Ltd
(a member of The Struik Publishing Group (Pty) Ltd)
Cornelis Struik House
80 McKenzie Street
Cape Town
8001

Reg. No.: 54/00965/07

First published in 1994

Text © Barbara Hey 1994
Photographs © Sheila Brandt 1994, with the exception of the following:
p. 2/3: Nancy Gardiner;
pp. 16, 18, 22: Struik Publishers;
pp. 31 (right), 37 (left), 53 (right), 59 (bottom left), 67 (right): Landmarks/Matthews;
p. 37 (right): Juan Espi;
p. 39: Barbara Hey;
pp. 51, 54: Marianne Alexander.

Illustrations © Struik Publishers 1994

All rights reserved. No part of this publication may be reproduced, stored in a
retrieval system, or transmitted, in any form or by any means, electronic, mechanical,
photocopying, recording or otherwise, without the prior written permission of the
copyright owners and publishers.

EDITING: Caroline Kingdon and Thea Coetzee
DESIGN: Petal Muller
DESIGN ASSISTANT: Lellyn Creamer
COVER DESIGN: Janice Evans
ILLUSTRATIONS: Jane Fenemore

Typesetting, Struik DTP
Reproduction by Unifoto (Pty) Ltd, Cape Town
Printed and bound by Tien Wah Press (Pte.) Ltd, Singapore

ISBN 1 86825 494 1

CONTENTS

CHAPTER ONE
GROWING HERBS 6

Planning 6
Soil and Site Preparation 6
Making Compost 8
Preparing Containers 9
Preparing a Raised Bed 9
Propagation and Planting 9
Caring for Herbs 11
Pest and Disease Control 11
Companion Planting with Herbs 13
Home Brews to Keep Herbs Healthy 14

CHAPTER TWO
DRYING, PRESERVING AND USING HERBS 16

Culinary Uses 16
Medicinal Uses 17
Cosmetic Uses 19
Fragrant Uses 20

CHAPTER THREE
DIRECTORY OF HERBS 23

Medicinal and Culinary Charts 76
Glossary 78
Index 80

CHAPTER ONE

GROWING HERBS

The term 'herbs' covers a wide range of plants – trees, shrubs, annuals, perennials, ground covers and even weeds.

Growing herbs can give endless pleasure and make for a better way of life, whether you have a large garden, live in a town house or have an apartment with only a windowsill or balcony. The adaptability of herbs enables them to be grown in an informal or formal garden, a vegetable plot, containers or among other plants in a bed or shrubbery.

PLANNING

Easy access is important when planning the size of beds and number of paths in a garden. To have to walk through a bed to cut herbs is a nuisance. People who have difficulty kneeling or bending or who use wheelchairs should consider a narrow, raised bed at a comfortable level alongside a smooth pathway. Ideally, culinary herbs should be planted next to the kitchen, although this is not always possible.

Wind, sun direction and frost are other factors to be considered. Hardy plants, like the taller varieties of rosemary, lavender, southernwood and some of the pelargonium family, are good windbreaks. For plants that cannot take very hot sun, take note of the sun's movement and grow where they are shaded by taller plants. Shield from frost by planting in a protected part of the garden and mulching roots in winter. Use low-growing herbs like creeping golden marjoram, pennyroyal, catmint, purslane, trailing rosemary and varieties of creeping thyme as ground covers. As well as being decorative and fragrant, they help to retain moisture and keep the soil cool in the heat of summer.

A bed of mixed herbs

For colour accents in the shrubbery or garden bed, plant bronze fennel, lavenders, curry bush, blue rosemaries, such as McConnell's Blue and Tuscany, golden tansy, santolina and rue. Curled parsley, purple basil and bush basil make attractive and useful border plants. Bright flowering herbs like pineapple sage, borage, nasturtium, roses, violets, calendula and yarrow, to name but a few, are also grown successfully among other garden plants.

To improve crops, herbs are often grown in the vegetable plot to keep the soil healthy and discourage pests (see **COMPANION PLANTING WITH HERBS** on page 13).

Another important factor to be considered before planting herbs out is the height and width of each herb. Do not make the mistake of planting small plants in the middle of the bed and tall plants in front.

When planning container planting, choose the size of container to suit the plant, bearing in mind that the roots need adequate space. Slow-growing plants such as bay trees should be put into pots suitable for their present size and transplanted after a year or two into containers which are slightly bigger.

Plenty of light is necessary for indoor plants on windowsills or elsewhere in the home. Beware of hot midday sun – it burns through glass. To accommodate more plants in a limited space, arrange wire plant pot holders down the sides of the window frames where curtains normally hang. Spray leaves regularly with lukewarm water to remove dust from indoor plants, either taking them outside or placing them on newspaper on the floor.

SOIL AND SITE PREPARATION

When preparing a new bed, dig down and turn the soil to about a spade's depth. Fork in compost, hoof-and-horn, bone meal and agricultural lime if indicated (quantities stated on bags). Rake over and remove any rough material such as matted roots and weeds. Water well before planting or sowing. When planting out into existing beds, add a little nourishment to each hole and work in well. For larger, woody-type plants, work a small handful of superphosphate into the soil. (Superphosphate is usually regarded as organic material.) Avoid using inorganic (chemical) fertilisers – although they promote lush growth, fragrance and flavour are often not as good as they should be.

A herb garden is the perfect place to spend a tranquil hour

This diagram shows clearly how the Three-Compartment Method works

Clayey and sandy soils improve with composting – it loosens and assists drainage in clayey soils and prevents leaching and retains moisture in sandy soils. For better water retention in sandy soil, keep the beds about 10 cm (4 in) lower than the surrounding paths or grass. Coarse sand may also be added to clayey soils which will assist with drainage when wet and prevent hard compacting in hot weather.

MAKING COMPOST

This is a way of returning to the earth some of what we take out of it. A gardener who makes compost and participates in a neighbourhood recycling scheme will have very little to put out for the municipal dump.

Material suitable for making compost ranges from crumpled, wet newspaper, cardboard, egg cartons, wine-bottle sleeves made from repulped paper, egg shells and dead floral arrangements to unseeded weeds, prunings cut into smaller pieces, leaves, grass cuttings and fruit and vegetable peelings. Potato peelings are only included if they are free of eelworm (nematode). Fresh manure – especially poultry manure or that from a pigeon loft – gives added nutriment and speeds up decomposition, as does the addition of dandelion, yarrow, nettle, comfrey or tansy. To test if a compost heap is working, insert an iron rod into the centre of the heap after a week and withdraw it after five minutes, when it should be hot to the touch. If not, loosen the heap to introduce more air. In more temperate climes, compost does not heat up as quickly. It is therefore best to chop the material very finely.

There are several methods of making compost. For a large garden the three-compartment method is tidy and satisfactory. A compost heap, the tumbler method or a commercial compost-maker are alternatives to consider, depending on the available space and practicability.

Three-Compartment Method

Make three adjoining compartments from wire, wooden slats or concrete slabs, leaving them open at the top and front. There should be gaps in the sides to allow for air circulation. Store all material except the manure in Bin 1. When there is sufficient material, make a bed of small twigs etc. in Bin 2, then layer the contents of Bin 1 with manure on top of this area. If there is soil available, spread a little between the layers. (I find enough soil remains on the roots of weeds and dead plants.) Take care to spread grass cuttings evenly otherwise they tend to become slimy. Moisten each layer and compact the material lightly.

Keep damp but not soggy. Cover in heavy rain because excess water will stop the natural heating action necessary for breakdown. After four weeks, or when the material begins to darken, fork contents of Bin 2 into Bin 3, spreading evenly and damping down if necessary. This could take any time from four weeks to many months, depending upon the air temperature, mix of materials and how finely they were chopped. Once the compost is a good, dark colour, and the contents are no longer recognisable, it should be ready and is best used within the next two or three months. Any

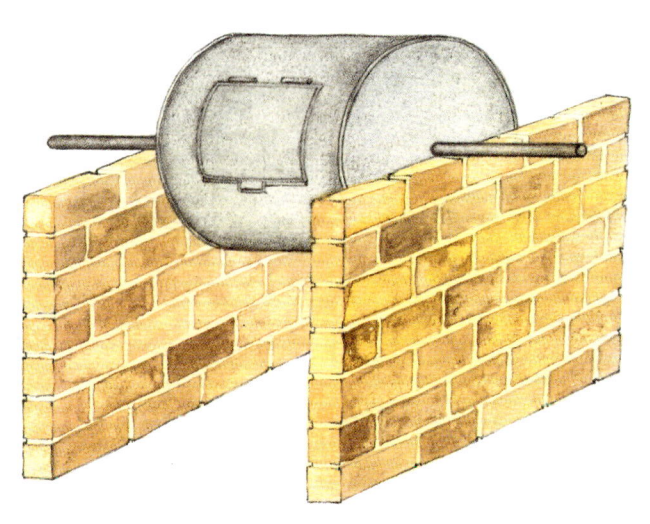

The Tumbler Method is a practical way of making compost

remaining coarse material is then tossed back into Bin 2. Now the material which has been collecting in Bin 1 is layered in Bin 2 and the cycle is repeated.

Compost Heap

Place coarse material, such as twigs, at the base of the heap and layer all material with any manure that is available. Damp down and cover with long grasses or straw. Turn and restack every six weeks until ready.

Tumbler Method

Cut an opening measuring 50 x 50 cm (20 x 20 in) in the middle of a 200-litre (45-gallon) drum. Hinge one edge and on the opposite side, solder a closure (like a hasp and staple) to form a flap that can be opened. Make an opening at each end of the drum and pass a strong rod through these openings to enable the drum to be rotated. Mount the 'tumbler' so that a wheelbarrow can be pushed underneath it. As material becomes available, put it into the drum through the hatch, with the odd handful of manure. Sprinkle with water if necessary. Turn the drum a few times after each addition. The inside heat (and that outside if the air is warm) should produce compost fairly quickly. Push a wheelbarrow under the drum, open the hatch and scrape the compost into the barrow, returning any material which has not yet decomposed.

Commercial Compost-Maker

This is suitable for a very small garden and can be obtained from major garden centres or nurseries.

Whichever method you use, don't forget to add at least one activating agent to the material while in the making. (Another natural method is to use 'recycled' beer!) Well-made compost should not smell or attract flies. When turning compost, look out for large, grey maggots. Destroy them as they turn into big, hard, black-and-yellow beetles which feed on roses and dahlias.

Herbs planted among paving stones

PREPARING CONTAINERS

If containers are placed under trees, raise them on bricks or tiles to keep the holes clear of the ground for proper drainage. Small, tender plants should be kept out of the drip area as raindrops damage them.

Containers should always have enough holes in the bottom to ensure effective drainage. First place a layer of broken clay pot, china or stones over the holes covering the bottom of the container. Now fill with prepared soil. Do not overfill as space is needed for watering. Use what soil is available and add compost and small quantities of other nutriment, as for garden soil. I find a wheelbarrow most useful for mixing the soil when filling containers.

Extra nourishment, especially for herbs in containers, is supplied by applying a seaweed or fish emulsion to the roots or using it as a foliar spray. The smell soon dissipates. Mix in the exact proportions as prescribed on the container.

PREPARING A RAISED BED

If raised beds are on a non-porous base, drainage holes must be made near the bottom of the wall. Place a good layer of broken clay pot, china, stones or broken brick at the bottom of the cavity, then coarse sand for a third of the depth before filling with a good soil mix. Leave room at the top to allow for watering.

PROPAGATION AND PLANTING

The most usual methods of propagating herbs are by sowing seeds, taking heel or tip cuttings, layering, dividing roots or growing from suckers.

Growing from Seed

This needs care and patience as some herbs, for example parsley, take up to three weeks to germinate. The viability of seed varies. Seed, like that of basil, keeps indefinitely, but some varieties need to be sown as soon as the seed is ripe. If this is not practicable, seeds may be kept in a sealed container in the freezer or in a dry, dark place.

The best sowing medium is a fine soil of which half should be sand. As it is not high in nutrients, the seeds grow strong roots in search of food.

SOWING IN TRAYS:
Water the soil in the trays well before sowing. For easier distribution of fine seed, mix with a little dry soil and then sow. Fine seed should only be covered with a fine dusting of soil. Larger seeds should be covered to twice their thickness. With a flat piece of wood or other suitable material, press the soil down firmly. Make sure that the trays are level and that the soil is evenly spread. Cover the trays with a single sheet of newspaper and glass. Check each morning, and as soon as the seeds germinate, remove the newspaper and cover the seedlings only

with the glass (which helps to retain moisture). Never allow the trays to dry out. Use a fine garden spray to water when necessary.

As the seedlings develop, remove the glass to allow more air and light to reach them. When they are at the four-to-six-leaf stage, lift them carefully (an old kitchen fork is useful), separate them and plant in deeper trays or small pots with good soil. Firm in gently and water with a fine spray or a sponge dipped in water and carefully squeezed around the seedlings. Gradually harden off by moving the plants into sunlight as they grow. When they look strong and healthy, plant out.

SOWING IN SITU:
Rake the ground level and at the same time remove any coarse material. Water well. Scatter seed or make long grooves; this latter method allows for even sowing and prevents overcrowding of seedlings. Grooves (or drills) are better for larger seeds.

A tip cutting

Most seeds sown in situ need to be protected from the elements in any way that is practicable. I use a fine shadecloth, anchored with bricks or stones. As the seedlings grow taller, the shadecloth is then raised by increasing the height of the brick piles. A more elaborate method is to use wooden frames and different gauges of shadecloth.

A heel cutting

Growing from Cuttings

A tip cutting is taken from the top of a fairly firm stem, just below a node. A heel cutting has a slightly ragged 'heel' when it is gently pulled from the parent plant.

To propagate you will require:

- sharp secateurs or a knife
- a general purpose hormone rooting powder
- a tray or pot of coarse sand
- a piece of thin cane or a knitting needle
- a watering can with a fine rose

The average length of a tip or heel cutting is 10 cm (4 in). Strip the leaves from the lower stem and if there is any bud formation, nip it out. Dip the cutting in water, shake, dip into rooting powder and tap off the excess. In the tray or pot, make a hole in the sand with the cane or knitting needle and plant the cutting. The closer the cuttings, the better the growth. If you only have a few cuttings, place them around the edge of the pot, not in the centre. Firm down and water. Keep in a warm, shady place. After five to six weeks, gently lift a few cuttings. If they have developed a root system, transplant them into deeper trays, pots or bags of good soil. Firm down and water. Gradually move the plants out into the sunshine to harden off and let them grow sturdy before planting them out.

Growing by Layering

For this method you will require:

- ❖ a sharp knife
- ❖ hormone rooting powder
- ❖ strong wire loops or half-bricks

Low-growing flexible branches are best for this method. Take the branch and make a small cut (not right through) about 30 cm (12 in) from the tip or where practicable. Dust with rooting powder. Carefully bend the branch (still attached to the mother plant) and bury the cut section in the ground, keeping the tip well exposed. Anchor the branch with wire loops or bricks. Keep well-watered. After a few months a root system should develop. Sever the new plant from the mother and leave it for a week to recover from the shock. Lift and plant out.

Layering

Growing by Root Division

Where indicated (see Chapter 3), lift plants in spring or autumn. Gently shake off soil and either prise apart or cut through the root system with secateurs. Each section should have both roots and foliage. Remove any old wood and dead leaves. Plant the sections in good soil either directly in the garden or in pots or bags.

Root division

Keep an eye on the plants and check their water requirements until they show new growth.

Growing from Suckers

When a sucker shows above the ground near a mature plant, expose the connecting root and cut through. Leave it in position, cover with soil, and water. Leave for at least a week when the sucker, which already has its own root system, should have recovered sufficiently to be lifted and bagged in good soil. When the sturdy, new growth appears, move it out into the garden.

CARING FOR HERBS

Dead flowers and foliage should be removed. Nip out growing tips and prune well to keep plants compact and bushy. Weeds should also be dug up regularly and composted before they go to seed.

Herbs can be killed as often by over-watering as by under-watering (for water requirements, see individual herbs in Chapter 3). To check container plants, stick a finger into the soil for about 3 cm (1 in) and water only if the soil is dry.

All herbs should be fed with an occasional spraying or watering of a seaweed or fish emulsion, diluted according to instructions on the container. Container plants will require more regular feeding. Perennials benefit from a twice-yearly dressing of compost into which some well-rotted manure has been mixed.

PEST AND DISEASE CONTROL

Natural methods of controlling pests are a must. Apart from the fact that one is eating from the garden, the ecological cycle must not be broken. Managing a garden this way means that no insect or bug is completely eliminated and thus the cycle is kept intact. The smallest to the largest creatures are part of the chain.

Fortunately herbs are susceptible to few pests and diseases, but one should watch out for:

ANTS: Outdoors, trace them back to their nests. Pour down or spray over the nest a solution of half Jeyes Fluid and half water. For the house or patio area, mix 5 ml (1 tsp) borax with 20 ml (4 tsps) sugar in 250 ml (½ pt) warm water. Pour this mixture into saucers, jam jar tops or any other shallow receptacles. Place them in strategic positions. The ants will partake of the liquid and then go back to their nests to die.

APHIDS: These black, green and orange pests cluster near the tips of plants and on the undersides of mature leaves. They suck the plants' sap and cause wilting. Spray with a soapy water solution every morning in order to suffocate the aphids. The breeding cycle must be broken so continue until no more appear – about three or four sprayings.

Aphid

Australian bug

AUSTRALIAN BUG OR COTTONY CUSHION SCALE: This is a soft-scale pest which lives off the sap of growing stems and is usually also found on the undersides of mature leaves and in the joints of woody stems. They cluster in a dirty white, woolly mass of ridged bodies with orangey-brown heads and they always attract ants. First deal with the ants, then brush off the 'bugs' with an old toothbrush dipped in a mixture of half methylated spirits and half water, or use one of the general garden sprays (see page 14).

CATERPILLARS: Pick these off by hand. Shake plants like mint and lemon balm to dislodge the small green caterpillars or use one of the general garden sprays (see page 14).

FUNGAL DISEASES: Mildew is one of these. Plants which do not have adequate sunshine are often affected. Dust with flowers of sulphur (vine dusting powder) early in the morning, when foliage is slightly moist from the dew, or try any one of the general garden sprays (see page 14). Badly infected foliage should be cut out and destroyed.

Pests and Diseases

Mildew

Rust

RED SPIDER: This is not a spider in the true sense of the word but a mite which lives on the undersides of leaves and thrives in hot, dry conditions. As a preventative, spray undersides of leaves of susceptible plants daily (see individual herbs in Chapter 3). If it occurs, use one of the garden sprays containing Jeyes Fluid (see page 14) or dust the undersides of leaves with flowers of sulphur (vine dusting powder).

Red spider

RUST: Bright orange markings appear on the foliage of herbs like mint and chives. If new stock is available, remove and destroy the old plants and plant new ones in a different position. Otherwise, spray with a mild commercial copper spray or try a Jeyes Fluid brew (see page 14). This is best done after all foliage is cut down near to ground level and plenty of compost applied as a mulch. Destroy all affected foliage.

SCALE: Hard, brown ovals appear on the undersides of leaves or on woody stems. Where there is scale there are ants, so look out for ants and deal with them (see page 11). If the plant is not too big, the scale can be removed by brushing with an old toothbrush dipped in a mixture of half water to half methylated spirits. A mature tree will need to be treated with a commercial oleum spray, to be repeated at the end of ten days.

Scale

SLUGS AND SNAILS: There are ways of ridding the garden of these pests by means other than poisons. If large cabbage leaves are left face down in the garden overnight there will be slugs and snails waiting to be disposed of in the morning. Half citrus peels containing a little beer and placed strategically prove effective traps. Walk round the garden in the evening or early morning with half a bucket of strong lime or salt water and drop snails into this solution to kill them off. To protect young seedlings, dip coarse string in Jeyes Fluid or creosote and lay it on the ground around the plants. Slugs and snails will not cross over the string. Commercial tobacco dust, sprinkled sparingly, is also a deterrent.

Snail

STINK BUGS OR SHIELD BUGS: They are hard-backed, grey bugs exuding a stinking fluid when touched. The younger bugs are brown. They cause extensive tip-wilting. A most effective way of dealing with them is to snip them in half as you go round the garden. Alternatively you can attach a firm piece of wood of 50 cm (20 in) long to a jam tin with a nail. Pour a little paraffin into the tin and slip it under the bug, knocking it into the paraffin with another length of wood. This works well as stinkbugs have a tendency to drop when disturbed. Lizards will eat them if they come into contact with them on the ground.

Stink bug

COMPANION PLANTING WITH HERBS

GOOD

Borage
All vegetables and especially strawberries.

Celery
Cauliflower, leeks, beans and celeriac.

Chervil
Radishes.

Chives
Carrots and especially apple trees and roses.

Comfrey
Most plants.

Cress (garden)
Radishes.

Dandelion
Helps to mature fruit and vegetables.

Dill
Most brassicas, particularly cabbage.

Elder
Most vegetables.

Feverfew
Controls aphid population on nearby plants.

Horseradish
Potatoes.

Lavender
All vegetables.

Lemon Balm
Most plants.

Lovage
All vegetables.

Marigold
Controls soil diseases, especially between tomatoes, aubergines and sweet green peppers.

Mint
Controls aphid population on nearby plants. Peppermint is beneficial to most plants. It particularly improves the quality of cabbage.

Nasturtium
Repels aphid from brassicas, especially broccoli, and benefits fruit trees.

Nettle
Stimulates growth in nearby plants and increases the essential oils in sage, oregano and peppermint.

Parsley
Tomatoes and roses.

Pennyroyal
Roses. Repels ants and makes a good border.

Rosemary
Most vegetables, especially the *Brassica* genus.

Sage
Stimulates growth of rosemary.

Santolina
Insect repellent, especially for spinach and lettuce.

Savory (summer)
Onions and green beans.

Savory (winter)
Insect repellent.

Southernwood
Controls aphid, especially on brassicas, and repels fruit fly.

Tansy
Repels fruit fly and fruit moth.

Tarragon
All vegetables.

Thyme
Good protective border for vegetable garden and helps to repel aphid and fruit moth.

Yarrow
Most plants, especially vegetables and medicinal herbs.

BAD

Basil
Dislikes rue.

Coriander
Hinders the seed formation of fennel.

Fennel
Grows badly near wormwood and is harmful to most plants, particularly beans, cucumber, tomatoes and caraway.

Savory (winter)
Inhibits the growth and germination of other seed (scatter plenty of seed).

Colourful herbs blend well with other plants to make a lovely mixed border

HOME BREWS TO KEEP HERBS HEALTHY

For these brews to be effective, they should be applied frequently as breeding cycles need to be broken. Keep an eye on the weather as a shower of rain within 24 hours of spraying will nullify your efforts. If you have a small garden, make up smaller quantities of the brews, but keep to the same proportions.

A Basic Spray using Jeyes Fluid

To 5 litres (10 pt) water add 10 ml (2 tsps) liquid seaweed extract and 5 ml (1 tsp) each of ammonia, Jeyes fluid, liquid soap or detergent and Epsom salts (dissolved in a little warm water). Mix well and spray plants regularly once a week for prevention of various diseases.

For a more potent spray which can be used fortnightly, to the above mixture add a pinch of permanganate of potash (Condy's crystals), 15 ml (1 tbsp) each of tobacco dust and vinegar and 10 ml (2 tsps) of liquid organic fertilizer.

General Insect Spray

Crush (or better still, cut up and blend in a food processor) three big cloves of unpeeled garlic and 90 ml (3½ fl oz) liquid paraffin. Place the resulting pulp in a bowl, cover and leave for 24 hours. Melt 15 ml (1 tbsp) grated, oil-based kitchen soap in 500 ml (1 pt) hot water. Combine both liquid mixtures. When cool, strain into a glass jar or bottle and seal. Keep in the fridge.

To use, dilute 30 ml (2 tbsps) of this solution in 2 litres (4 pt) of cold water. Spray fortnightly.

Red Pepper Spray

Chop one large onion and one head of garlic, both unpeeled. Simmer with 15 ml (1 tbsp) cayenne pepper in 1½ litres (3 pt) of water for 20 minutes. Cool the mixture and strain into bottles. Seal and leave to stand for six weeks.

To spray, mix 15 ml (1 tbsp) of the mixture with 750 ml (1½ pt) of water. Use as required as a general anti-pest spray. It is particularly effective against caterpillars.

Comfrey Foliar Feed

Before comfrey flowers, cut as much of the herb as you can and pack it into an old bucket or similar container with holes in the bottom. Place a plate or tin lid on top and weight it down with half a brick. Put a plastic plant pot in an old basin and stand the bucket on the pot. After about three weeks there should be a quantity of brown fluid in the basin. Strain this and bottle it.

Spray on plants in the proportion of 15 ml (1 tbsp) comfrey liquid to 1 litre (2 pt) of water and a few drops of liquid detergent. (Put the remaining contents of the bucket onto the compost heap.)

There are many other brews using herbs like calendula, Inca marigold (khaki weed), nasturtium, nettle, southernwood, rue and tansy. Most brews are improved with the addition of dissolved soap or liquid detergent. This ingredient acts as a wetting agent which enables the spray to stick to the foliage.

Herbs such as origanum, bronze fennel and yarrow make a pretty border as a foreground for a wall of roses

CHAPTER TWO

DRYING, PRESERVING & USING HERBS

The best time of day to harvest herbs for drying is mid-morning, after any early morning moisture has evaporated and before the midday heat causes the volatile oils to dissipate. Flowers and foliage are either tied into small, loose bunches and hung up to dry or spread out onto paper or drying racks.

If foliage is for culinary use, the dust should be rinsed off and water shaken free. When hanging herbs or placing them on racks, cover with muslin or similar material to keep them dust-free. Hang away from sunlight but *not* in a garage because of exhaust fumes. Kitchens may also be too steamy. (I seldom dry foliage for culinary use, as fresh herbs are nearly always available.)

Drying racks can be simple frames of wood covered with wire mesh and stacked on top of each other. A more elaborate form of rack is one which is mounted on pulleys to be hoisted up to the ceiling, out of the way. This will also provide somewhere to hang bunches of herbs.

When drying seeds for germinating, cut heads with stems and put them headfirst into a paper bag with the stems sticking out of the opening. Make a few small holes in the sides of the bag for air to circulate. Tie the neck of the bag with string and hang up for the seeds to dry. They usually drop into the bag or are gently rubbed off the stems.

To remove insects or foreign matter from seeds to be dried for culinary use, hold the stems of the seed heads and dip them in boiling water. Shake gently to remove moisture before hanging them in paper bags. Once the seeds are perfectly dry, remove the husks and store in airtight containers away from the light.

Herbs have many culinary uses

Many herbs freeze well. Wash the leaves, chop them and freeze with a little water in ice cube trays. Remove from trays and store in small bags in the freezer. Use as required in stews, soups, etc. Basil leaves can be frozen. First brush with cooking oil and then wrap in freezer paper.

CULINARY USES

The recipes and suggestions given here are merely a guide, as the use of herbs in cooking is very much a matter of relying on one's own taste and instincts. Remember less is better than more – it is easy to add to a recipe but almost impossible to take out. Have fun experimenting!

Bouquet Garni

This is usually made up of a bay leaf, two sprigs of thyme and three of parsley, tied together with a length of thread. The thread makes it easier to remove the herbs from the dish before serving. Other herbs like sweet marjoram and sage are sometimes added to bouquet garni.

Herb Butters

Finely chop suitable herbs and blend into the butter with a little lemon juice. Roll into a sausage shape, wrap and store in the fridge. To use, slice and top grilled fish and meat or baked potatoes. The same butter is also used on sliced French bread which is wrapped in foil and crisped in a hot oven. For easier serving, slice the bread right through and assemble on the foil when buttered. Spread extra butter over the top of the loaf before wrapping.

Capers

For 'poor man's' capers, pick young, green nasturtium seeds and soak them in salt water for a few hours. Rinse and pack in small glass jars. Boil a good wine or grape vinegar with herbs and spices, strain and fill the jars while still hot. Seal tightly. Leave for one month before using.

Pick nasturtium buds (these are even more like real caper buds) just before or as they start to colour. Cover with coarse salt and leave for 12 hours. Rinse and place in a tea towel, gather the ends of the towel together and shake until dry. Pack in jars and proceed as for seeds.

Cottage Cheese

Chop herbs of your choice and blend into the cheese with salt, pepper and a squeeze of lemon juice. Add chopped, sweet red pepper which has been patted dry in paper towelling. Do not dry the pepper if the cheese is to be used as a dip, as this mixture needs to be thinner. For spreading purposes, try to find a firm brand of cheese. Low-fat or full-cream cheeses are equally good.

Crystallizing

The easiest way to crystallize rose petals, violet or borage flowers and mint leaves, is to lightly beat egg white and coat petals and leaves. Use a small paintbrush, or if dipping into egg white, take care not to overdo it. Dust lightly with castor sugar and lay them on to waxed paper on biscuit trays. They can be sun-dried but drying in a cool oven is best. When crisp, lift off the paper and store in an airtight container.

Angelica requires a different method. Ideally, stems should be as thick as one's thumb, though I have also used thinner ones. Cut the stems into workable-sized pieces. Cook gently until just tender, then drain. With a sharp knife remove the paper-thin outer skin. Weigh the stems. For each 500 g (1 lb) of stems you will need 500 g (1 lb) sugar and 250 ml (½ pt) water. Lay the stems in a dish and cover with the sugar. Leave for 48 hours. Now pour the resulting syrup plus water and stems into a saucepan. Stirring gently, simmer until the stems are clear and all the syrup is absorbed. Lift and place stems on a rack in a cool oven until crisp on the outside. Store in an airtight container.

Fines Herbes

This is a finely chopped combination of equal parts of chervil, chives, parsley and tarragon and is a most delicious seasoning for omelettes.

Mint Sauce

Chop about 30 ml (2 tbsps) crinkle-leaved spearmint (*M. rotundifolia*) or spearmint (*M. spicata*) with about 10 ml (2 tsps) sugar. Stir in 15 ml (1 tbsp) hot water, then add about 45 ml (3 tbsps) of a good vinegar. Serve cold with mutton or lamb.

Pesto

In a blender or food processor, combine 30 g (1 oz) basil leaves and flowers, 30 g (1 oz) finely grated Parmesan cheese, 30 g (1 oz) pine nuts or walnuts, 3 cloves of garlic, 45 ml (3 tbsps) olive oil and 30 ml (2 tbsps) hot water. This may be kept in a closed container in the fridge. Add to pasta or vegetables.

Pistou

In a blender or food processor, combine 30 g (1 oz) fresh basil leaves and flowers, 60 g (2 oz) Parmesan cheese, 4 cloves of garlic and 45 ml (3 tbsps) olive oil. This may be kept in a closed container in the fridge. Add to pasta or vegetables.

Ravigoti

Chop equal parts of chervil, chives, salad burnet, capers and tarragon. Sprinkle the mixture over pasta, baked potatoes or cold meat.

Rose Jam

Collect the darkest and most highly scented rose petals that are available. *N.B. Do not use petals from bushes which have been sprayed with chemical pesticides.* Remove bitter cream bases of the petals. For every 500 g (1 lb) petals, you will need about 500 g (1 lb) white sugar, 500 ml (1 pt) water and 45 ml (3 tbsps) lemon juice. Use a large saucepan, as this jam tends to froth up. In order to prevent the jam from boiling over, take a knob of butter and rub it around the inside rim of the saucepan. (Drop the remaining butter into the saucepan.)

Rinse the petals and drain. Simmer the petals with the water until soft. Draw the saucepan off the heat and stir in the lemon juice and sugar, stirring constantly until the sugar has dissolved. Return to the stove and cook for about 30 minutes, until it begins to thicken. Taste, and if more flavour is required, stir in 15 ml (1 tbsp) rose-water or 2.5 ml (½ tsp) citric acid. Put a saucer in the fridge to chill. Bring the jam to a rapid boil. Test to see if it has set by pouring a little on to the chilled saucer and leaving it for a few minutes. When cool, run a fingertip through it. If it wrinkles the jam is ready. Remove from heat and allow to stand for a few minutes. Pour into warm, sterile jars and screw on caps while hot. Average yield: two 500 g (1 lb) jars.

Vinegars and Oils

For a base, use a pure wine or grape vinegar (not blended) and maize or sunflower oil. Vinegars and oils for culinary use are made in the same way. Pack a wide-mouthed glass jar three quarters full of the fresh herb or herbs of your choice. Fill the jar with either vinegar or oil. Cover with plastic film. (Lids become mucky or rusty.) Leave vinegars in the sun for about a week. Oils are better left out of the sun for about 10 days. (The heat of the sun could make the oil rancid.) Strain through muslin or old, clean tights and squeeze out every drop. Collect attractive bottles and place a few sprigs of an appropriate herb in each bottle and fill with the herbal vinegar or oil.

MEDICINAL USES

N.B. Serious and deep-seated health problems should not be treated from the herb garden. A correct diagnosis and treatment, properly supervised by a doctor practising complementary medicine, or a fully qualified and registered homeopath or naturopath, is essential. However, there are many simple and harmless herb treatments for minor health problems, bearing in mind the possibility of allergic reactions.

Herbs can be used to make delicious herb oils and vinegars as well as fragrant sachets and a tussie mussie

Calendula Cream/Ointment

Pharmacies do stock these, but if making your own, you will need aqueous cream or Vaseline as a base. (Vaseline leaves an oily film on the skin so is better for nappy rash as the aqueous cream soaks in too quickly.) Chop calendula stalks, stems and flowers. The proportion is roughly one part herb to three parts base. Gently melt the base in a saucepan and stir in the chopped herb. Draw to one side and leave for 24 hours. Heat again until just runny, then strain through muslin, squeezing out all the cream/ointment. Pour into sterile jars and seal. Aqueous-based creams have a limited life unless kept in the fridge.

Comfrey Cream/Ointment

Follow the same method as for *Calendula Cream/Ointment* above.

Herbal Tea or Tisane

Take the herb or herbs of your choice (quantities stated under appropriate herbs in Chapter 3). Pour boiling water over them and allow to stand for five minutes. Honey and lemon may be added to enhance the flavour.

Horehound Cough Sweets

Simmer a handful of horehound, three sprigs of peppermint and four rose pelargonium leaves in 250 ml (½ pt) water for 10 minutes. Strain when cool. Pour 125 ml (4 fl oz) of this liquid into a heavy saucepan. Add 15 ml (1 tbsp) each honey and lemon juice, 30 ml (2 tbsps) butter and 400 g (14 oz) sugar.

Stir until dissolved and boil for about five minutes, until it reaches the soft-ball stage. (Drop a little of the mixture into a cup of cold water. If ready, it will form a soft ball. Alternatively, use a sugar thermometer.) Remove the saucepan from the heat and beat until thick. Pour out on to a greased dish. When nearly cool, mark into squares with a sharp knife. When cold, break up and store in an airtight container.

Poultices

Use boiling water to heat herbs for poultices. As a precaution against skin irritation, cover the area with a thin film of Vaseline or a piece of muslin or gauze before applying.

COSMETIC USES

There are many recipes for homemade cosmetics, but most of these contain a higher proportion of bought ingredients than home-grown ones. I feel they are not worth the effort, especially as they tend to have such a short shelf life.

Herbal Bath

Herbs may be introduced into the bath water in several ways. The simplest is to cut a handful of a suitable herb or herbs (see the individual herbs in Chapter 3), tie them loosely in muslin or old, clean tights and then hang the bag from the hot water tap so that the water flows over the herbs. Oats or bran can also be added to this bag. When you are in the bath, use it as a body rub. After bathing, hang the bag to dry as it can be used more than once if there is fragrance.

Another method is to pour boiling water over the herbs in a basin. Leave them to steep until cold, strain and pour the liquid into the bath water. If you prefer to shower, take a basin of herb water and use it to sponge down after your shower, before leaving the cubicle. For this you may want a tepid brew.

Bath Vinegars and Oils

These are refreshing and soothing. To make your own, you will require an oil base such as technical or almond oil, and for a vinegar base, you can use any good grape or wine vinegar. Cut any fragrant herbs and pack them into a wide-mouthed jar until it is three quarters full. Top up with oil or vinegar. Cover the jar with plastic film and stand in a sunny position for 7 to 10 days.

Strain the mixture through muslin or old, clean tights and squeeze out every drop. Pour into pretty bottles with a sprig or two of herbs. (To prevent the oil marking the labels, seal them with clear nail varnish or a lacquer spray.) Use 30 ml (2 tbsps) oil or 60 ml (4 tbsps) vinegar for the average bath.

For an exotic bath, float rose petals in the water and add rose-water or a few drops of rose oil.

Essential oils also make a fragrant bath. They are strong so only use a few drops at a time. Purchase from a pharmacy or health shop.

Cosmetic and Fragrant Uses

Herbs have many fragrant uses, including making potpourri

Creams

These creams are used to soften the skin. (See **Calendula** and **Comfrey Cream/Ointment** under MEDICINAL USES on page 19).

Facial Steam

Before you start, tie back your hair and cleanse your face. Put two handfuls of any appropriate herb (see individual herbs in Chapter 3) into a heatproof basin. Pour 1 litre (2 pt) of boiling water over the herbs. Bend over and cover your head and the basin with a large towel. Steam the face for 10 minutes to open pores, remove impurities and allow the volatile herbal oils to work. Make sure that the basin is at a level where you can sit comfortably. After steaming, rinse your face with cold water and pat on a face tonic. This facial steam can be used once a week for an average skin, less often for dry skin and more frequently for oily skin.

Face Tonics

Find details under the listed herbs in Chapter 3. Rose-water is used as a face tonic and is purchased from a pharmacy or health shop.

Hair Rinses

Find details under the appropriate listed herbs in Chapter 3.

FRAGRANT USES

In bygone times when cleanliness was not regarded as important, herbs were used to disguise odours and counteract the spread of germs. Strewing herbs over floors and rush mats was one way of doing this.

Potpourri

This is a comparatively simple way of introducing the fragrance of herbs to the home. To make it, you will need to collect and dry scented flowers for fragrance as well as some pretty ones for colour. The combination of scents and colours is a matter of availability and personal choice.

When drying rose petals, include some leaves as they turn a lovely soft shade of green.

Any dried sweet- or spicy-scented foliage should be stripped from the stems, which are then discarded.

Spices such as anise, cinnamon and cloves are often added to mixtures of herbs for potpourri. They also help to 'fix' the scent. Other fixatives include chopped or minced and dried citrus pith and peel. After squeezing the fruit, collect the peels and store them in plastic bags in the freezer until you have enough to make a worthwhile amount. Mince or chop the peel finely and spread it out on trays to dry in the sun or in a cool oven. When evenly and crisply dry (not frizzled), store the peel in closed jars until required.

Whole coriander seed and the leaves of the Inca marigold (khaki weed) can also act as a fixative and be used to hold the volatile oils.

In many potpourri recipes the use of orris root is advocated. This is the powdered root of the Florentine iris. It may be purchased but is sometimes difficult to find and a good powder can be expensive.

Essential oils are added for long-lasting fragrance. As these are expensive, buy only two or three of those that appeal to you and will complement the herbs being used.

To Mix:
Spread an old cotton sheet on the floor and pile on pretty and fragrant flowers and foliage. Tip the chopped peel on top, as well as any spices you may be using. Add the oil to the peel drop by drop. The oils are concentrated so do not waste them by

being over-generous. Stir with your hands to blend ingredients. Pack into a large glass or pottery container, seal and leave to mature for four or five days. Open and test for fragrance. If not strong enough, tip out on to the sheet and add some more peel with a little oil. Blend together and repack in the jar. It will be ready to use in a fortnight.

Potpourri is put into pretty pots or jars with lids and placed around the house away from sunlight. Leave jars open when fragrance is desired and close when away from home to preserve the scent. (Do not wash the now-fragrant sheet but fold it and put it away for future use.)

PROPORTIONS:
To six to eight lightly packed cups of dried material add 1 cup of dried peel and 10 drops of oil, depending on the strength of the oil.

OTHER USES:
For *anti-moth sachets and bags*, the potpourri mixture must include a fair proportion of herbs like lavender, bay, marigold, santolina or southernwood, all of which repel moths. This same mixture is also ideal for *padded coathangers*.

The mixture used for a *sleep-pillow* should have a higher proportion of chamomile and/or lavender.

To make sachets and bags, use a thin, pretty cotton fabric. For the linen cupboard or placing between folded clothes, make flat sachets. Bags should have ribbons long enough for hanging.

When using potpourri in sleep-pillows or coathangers, pad out and soften with a proportion of polyester stuffing. Be generous with the herbs. Make casings of plain cotton to hold the blended stuffing, stitch up and cover prettily. It is advisable to use washable covers for pillows.

For fragrance in the house, I put a handful of suitable herbs in the bag of the *vacuum cleaner*. The scent is given off as the air passes through the machine. If using a *tumble drier*, tie a handful of herbs in old, clean tights and toss in with the clothes. A few dried herbs under the *ironing blanket* make the task more pleasant. For a *dinner table centrepiece*, make an arrangement of herbs instead of the usual flowers.

Tussie Mussie

As a gift, especially for someone in hospital, a tussie mussie is ideal. It is a posy made up of about a hundred stems of herbs and, when it begins to fade after a week in water, the stems are mopped dry and it is hung upside down until crispy dry. It becomes a pretty, long-lasting, fragrant decoration for a table or may be hung in a cupboard or wardrobe.

To make it you will need:

- sharp scissors
- secateurs
- florists' tape
- 1 m (1 yd) ribbon
- a small glass jar or vase
- one rosebud or carnation flower
- ten stems each of at least eight different herbs

Among the most suitable herbs are various lavender flowers and foliage, rosemary, rose, lemon and peppermint pelargonium leaves, santolina flowers and foliage, mints and thymes in flower and flowers and foliage of marjoram and oregano or any herb you may find suitable. To add extra softness to the posy I often include the flowers of parsley, celery or fennel.

Cut 15 cm (6 in) stems and strip off foliage to 5 cm (2 in) from the top (save this to dry for potpourri).

Cut 4 cm (1 ½ in) pieces of florists' tape on a slant, then take, for example, a lavender flower and a stem of santolina foliage and bind these together with a piece of tape. Prepare all the herbs in the same way, except the pelargonium leaves and the rosebud.

To form the centre, bind four or five small rose- or lemon-scented pelargonium leaves evenly around the rosebud. Arrange the pairs of herbs in circles of the same combinations around the centrepiece.

As posy-holders are sometimes difficult to obtain, I usually finish off the tussie mussie with a circle of approximately six large peppermint or rose pelargonium leaves. Tape the posy well and tie it with ribbon, making an attractive bow.

Trim the stems and slip into a vase of water. Change the water daily.

A tussie mussie makes a fragrant and unusual gift

A wide variety of herbs can be dried and used in combination with petals to make sweet-smelling potpourri

CHAPTER THREE
DIRECTORY OF HERBS

In this book I've written about herbs which are most easily obtained, comparatively hassle-free to grow and are of use in our daily lives. In my own small suburban garden at 'The Herb House', I grow well over 400 species and varieties of herbs. Nowadays some of these plants are only of historical interest or can only be used safely if they are correctly processed. May you gain pleasure from your gardening, meet friendly fellow growers in your quest for herbs to add to your collection and experience the joy of taking home and nurturing new varieties.

ANGELICA

Angelica archangelica

Origin

Far northern Europe.

Culinary Uses

Angelica has a sweet, refreshing fragrance. Leaves may be chopped for fruit salad and also added to fish dishes and cottage cheese in small quantities. Cook angelica leaves and stems with sour fruit like apricots, plums and rhubarb to neutralize their acidity. Stems boiled with jams improve flavour, but remove the stems before bottling. Steam the stems as a vegetable. Young stems may be used as a substitute for salad celery. The strong-flavoured seeds are added in small quantities to breads, biscuits and cakes.

For crystallizing angelica, spring is the best time to cut the mature stems, roughly the thickness of your thumb (see page 17).

Angelica

Medicinal Uses

A tea made of angelica leaves or a small amount of powdered root has a calming effect. Coughs and colds are also relieved by drinking the tea. To relieve indigestion, nibble a stalk of angelica.

Other Uses

For a refreshing bath, add leaves and stems to the water. Leaves and seeds may be dried for potpourri. **N.B. Angelica archangelica *is not to be confused with the ornamental variety,* A. pachycarpa.**

Cultivation

Choose the coolest part of the garden. The soil needs to be deep, rich, slightly acid and moist but at the same time well-drained, as soggy soil will cause dieback. Protect plants from the wind. Angelica does not seem to do well under trees so a position against a fence or wall with some morning sun is best. To perpetuate the plant, it is necessary to cut out the flowering stem, which usually shoots up in the second year and may be used for crystallizing. Allow to flower in the third or fourth year when the plant will need to be replaced. Propagate angelica from seed which should be sown in trays

Angelica archangelica

Height 60 cm (24 in) or more. Spread 60 cm (24 in). Angelica has hollow, ribbed stalks with branching stems of bright green, basal leaves which divide into finely serrated, oval leaflets. Leaves are smooth and greyish on the underside. Large umbels of green/white or yellow flowers appear on upright stems. Seeds are ribbed and green to light brown when ripe.

or in situ as soon as possible after removing them from the plant. If this is not practicable, seal the seed in a plastic container and store it in the fridge, as angelica seed soon loses its viability. Annual sowing is advisable in order to ensure continuity. Plant out the seedlings when they have four to six leaves. Do not leave them too long before transplanting, as they have long taproots.

Pests

Red spider. Water the undersides of the leaves, especially in hot, dry weather, as a preventative. At the first signs of yellowing and silvering of leaves, dust them with flowers of sulphur. To make it stick, do this early in the morning when the leaves are still slightly damp.

BASIL

Most commonly used varieties are:
Ocimum basilicum (sweet basil)
O. basilicum purpurascens (purple or opal basil)
O. crispum (lettuce basil)
O. minimum (bush basil)

Sweet basil

Purple basil

Origin

India and Egypt. Many forms are also found in different climates.

Culinary Uses

Basil has a warm, resinous, clove-like flavour and fragrance. Flowers and leaves have many culinary uses and are best used fresh and added only during the last few minutes of cooking. For any dish with tomato, like salad, soup, pizza and pasta, it is a must. Finely chopped basil stirred into mayonnaise makes a good sauce for fish. Use as a garnish for vegetables, chicken and egg dishes. Large leaves of lettuce basil are used to envelop various foods as one would use vine leaves. Tear rather than chop basil for salads.

Oils and vinegars are also excellent mediums for conveying flavour to food (see page 17). At the height of the growing season, make pesto and pistou (see page 17) and freeze in small containers for use in winter. It does not dry well for cooking but leaves may be layered with salt and

Bush basil

kept in a crock in a cool place for use in winter. (Take care to rinse off all the salt before using the leaves.) Leaves can also be frozen by brushing them with oil and wrapping them in freezer paper. Alternatively, try a perennial basil of which there are different types, but which are not all suitable for culinary use.

Medicinal Uses

A strong solution of leaves in boiling water makes an effective mouthwash for treating sore gums or ulcers. Use every half hour or whenever one remembers. When possible, tuck a leaf down next to the ulcer.

Other Uses

Basil added to the bath is refreshing. Leaves and flowers may be dried for scenting potpourri and seed for germinating. Cut flower heads as they mature (or run fingers down the stems to remove the flowers). Dry until crisp. Burn sprigs of basil on barbecue fires to deter mosquitoes. A bunch hung in the kitchen or a pot of basil on the windowsill will also help to deter flies.

Ocimum basilicum

Height 45 cm (18 in). This is a bushy plant with stiff, branching stems producing glossy, bright green, ovate leaves with short stalks. Spikes of small white flowers grow in circles above the foliage.

Ocimum minimum

Height 45 cm (18 in). This is similar to *Ocimum basilicum* but its smaller leaves are denser on the stalk. There is a dwarf variety, round in shape with very dense foliage and tiny white flowers. Height 15–20 cm (6–8 in).

Ocimum basilicum purpurascens

Height 30 cm (12 in). This variety is a most attractive plant with shiny, ovate, purple leaves, almost black at times and at others blotched with green. The spikes of flowers are pinky mauve.

Ocimum crispum

Height 50 cm (20 in). This is one of the tall, vigorous varieties with large, crinkled, serrated, bright green leaves which have the habit of curling back on themselves.

Cultivation

Basil is an annual requiring good, well-drained soil in a warm position. It is a good container plant, also suitable for a windowsill. In very hot climates, basils tend to droop and should then be gently hosed down. Seed may be sown continuously from October right through to late summer in situ or in trays. Germination is rapid. Transplant when four leaves appear. When settled in, nip out centre stem to promote bushing. Continuous picking prolongs the life of the herb. Seed collected from your garden does not always germinate true to form as hybridization takes place readily.

Pests

Slugs and snails (see page 12).

BAY

Laurus nobilis

Origin

Mediterranean countries.

Bay

Culinary Uses

Bay has a spicy fragrance and flavour. Most fish, meat and chicken dishes are improved with the addition of bay leaves. They are also used to impart flavour to marinades, soups, stews and custards. Bay has a strong flavour, so use it with discretion. It is one of the ingredients of *bouquet garni* and pickling spice. Use fresh or dried but check for and remove scale from undersides of leaves. Never use immature, droopy leaf tips as they shrivel, lack fragrance and have a high hydrocyanic acid content. Cut branches of mature leaves to hang, or dry individual leaves on racks.

Laurus nobilis

Height up to 10 m (30 ft) if not clipped. The bark of this tree is smooth and has a reddish-green colour. The leaves are dark green, leathery and ovate. Some bay trees have less dense foliage than others and slightly elongated leaves. The small, insignificant flowers appear at the base of the leaf stem. These turn into hard, green berries which eventually become purple.

Other Uses

To prevent damage by silverfish, place bay leaves in drawers or bookcases. When storing dried legumes, cereals, pasta or rice, a few leaves in their containers keep away weevils.

Cultivation

Bay trees will take full sun but need shelter in areas of frost. Prepare the ground well with compost, bone meal and a handful of superphosphate. For a container, mix a smaller quantity of nourishment with the soil and compost. Bay trees are adaptable and can be kept well-clipped for container culture. They also make a good hedge. Propagate from heel cuttings taken in autumn or spring, although they do not take readily. Older trees may sucker. These suckers can be severed from the tree and left in the ground for a few weeks to recover from shock. Carefully dig out and plant in bags of good soil until well-grown. This takes time so it might be worthwhile purchasing a tree from a nursery.

Diseases

Bay is subject to sooty mildew and scale. On a small tree the scale can be removed by brushing with an old toothbrush dipped into a mixture of half methylated spirits and half water. Larger trees will need to be treated with an oleum spray.

BERGAMOT

Monarda didyma

Origin

North America.

Culinary Uses

Bergamot has a savoury, fruity aroma. Use flowers and chopped young leaves in salad, fruit salad and fruit drinks. Improve any pork dish with the addition of bergamot leaves during cooking. Freeze the chopped leaves with water in ice trays or place single flowers in ice cube compartments, slowly pour water over them and freeze. Make a tea with five or six large, fresh leaves or 5 ml (1 tsp) crushed, dried leaves to 250 ml (½ pt) boiling water. Dried bergamot leaves are also added to Indian or Ceylon tea.

Bergamot

Medicinal Uses

Bergamot tea soothes a sore throat if sipped warm, and relieves nausea and flatulence. To loosen the phlegm of a chesty cough, pour boiling water over ten large leaves in a small basin and put the basin in a paper bag. Gather the neck of the bag around the nose and mouth and inhale for as long as is comfortable.

Other Uses

Use the leaves to make a facial steam which is suitable for all types of skin. Leaves and flowers may be dried for colour and fragrance in potpourri by cutting flowers and foliage on long stems in late sum-

Monarda didyma

Height 60 cm (24 in). Bergamot has strong, slightly hairy, square stems. The heads of narrow, tubular flowers which appear in the form of a whorl on single stems, are usually bright red. These flowers appear in midsummer. The flowers can also range in colour from pink to mauve. The oval, green leaves grow in pairs and are slightly rough.

mer, tying in bunches and hanging up. Fresh or dried flowers are useful for arrangements. Bergamot is a colourful garden plant.

Cultivation

This herb is a perennial growing from clumps of rooted runners. Propagate it by root division in spring or cuttings in summer. It is necessary to lift and divide every two to three years. Break up clumps and discard the old, woody growth. Plant in sun or semi-shade in a rich, light soil with the addition of bone meal. At the end of summer, cut back to the small, reddish leaves near the ground. Bergamot is most suitable for container planting.

BORAGE

Borago officinalis
(Herb of joy)

Origin

Southern and southwestern Europe.

Borage

Culinary Uses

Borage is cucumber flavoured. The flowers and young leaves are added to salads, dips and cucumber soup. For a most attractive addition to summer drinks, carefully place the flowers in ice cube compartments, slowly pour water over them and freeze. Chop leaves and add to soups and stews during the last few minutes of cooking. Improve pale, uninteresting cabbage by cooking one part borage leaves with two parts cabbage. The leaves can be cooked like spinach as a separate vegetable. The hairiness goes with chopping and cooking. Flowers are a pretty garnish. Borage is not a suitable herb to be dried for cooking purposes but one may crystallize the flowers for decorating cakes and desserts when fresh flowers are not available (see page 17).

Medicinal Uses

For a quick pick-me-up, make a tea of a few flowers and leaves. For a blood-purifying and cough treatment, pour 625 ml (1¼ pt) boiling water over 125 ml (½ cup) roughly cut leaves. Drink as needed.

Other Uses

Borage makes a good facial steam for dry, sensitive skins. Dry flowers face down on paper to add colour to a potpourri mixture.

Borago officinalis

Height 80 cm (32 in). A thick, hollow stem grows from a rosette of dimpled, hairy, oval, dark green leaves with pointed tips. As the stem grows, the leaves are smaller and looser. These stems bear sprays of bright, true blue, star-shaped flowers with pointed, black stamens circled in white. Pink- and white-flowering varieties and those with variegated foliage do exist, but they are rare.

Cultivation

Borage is an annual. It is not fussy, but the better the soil, the more lush the growth, especially in a sunny, sheltered position. Sow seed in situ throughout the year except in very wet conditions. Borage self-sows freely. Transplant seedlings when young, but allow fairly close growth so that plants can support each other. This is necessary as growth tends to be lax.

BULBINE

Bulbine frutescens

Origin

Southern Africa.

Bulbine

Medicinal Uses

A first-aid plant, bulbine is a ready antidote for bee or other insect stings and bites, especially when outdoors. It helps to counteract the pain of bluebottle stings suffered when swimming or walking on the beach. The mucilaginous sap from broken bulbine leaves is also used to heal cold sores and chapped lips and to ease and heal burns. The sap is soothing when it is applied to a sunburnt skin.

Bulbine frutescens

Bulbine is a low-growing herb, and it is indigenous to South Africa. The leaves, which are firm, narrow, slightly flattened and succulent, grow directly from the crown. The slender stems bear small, cone-like heads of orange and yellow flowers.

Cultivation

It is a perennial which grows in full sun in average to poor soil. Bulbine grown in a pot near the kitchen door is a good idea in case of urgent need. It is ideal for hot, dry places where nothing much else will grow. Grow it from a rooted section taken from a mature plant, or an unrooted section which will soon root when potted. Plants will need water in very hot, dry weather. When a plant becomes dense and looks overcrowded, lift, divide and plant out.

CALENDULA

Calendula officinalis

Origin

Southern Europe.

Calendula

Culinary Uses

Flowers have a lightly spicy, tangy flavour. The merit of the culinary use of this herb is for eye appeal as the flavour is mild. Petals are separated carefully from the flower heads (they bruise easily) and used as an inexpensive substitute for saffron. Use in rice dishes, custards, stews, soups, cheese dips and salads.

Medicinal Uses

The leaves, stems and flowers have long been used for their healing properties. Calendula ointment (either bought or home-made, see page 19) is highly recommended for healing leg ulcers, varicose veins, bedsores and nappy rash. Oil of Calendula, obtainable from a pharmacy, is used on chilblains and cracked nipples. To staunch bleeding from a cut, crush any part of a calendula plant and hold it against the wound for a few minutes.

Other Uses

Flowers steeped in boiling water make a brightening rinse for fair hair. Calendula is decorative both in the garden and as a cut flower. To brighten potpourri, carefully remove the petals from the flower heads and spread them out to dry.

Calendula officinalis

Height 30–50 cm (12–20 in). This plant has brittle stems, branching with bright green, stalkless, oval to oblong leaves which, like the buds, are covered with slightly sticky, fine hairs. Of the daisy family, the large double and single flowers come in shades of palest yellow to deep orange. In some varieties the firm centres are dark brown. There are dwarf varieties which are suitable for edging and also for containers.

Cultivation

Calendula is an annual. Sow in situ or in trays. Germination is rapid – transplant at four- to six-leaf stage. Sow from early autumn into winter in the southern hemisphere, where calendula flowers in winter. Sow in spring and summer in the northern hemisphere where it will flower most of the year if the weather is mild. This herb needs good, well-drained soil in a sunny position. Water during hot spells.

Pests and Diseases

Watch out for caterpillars and hand-pick them from the plants. Dust with flowers of sulphur at the first sign of mildew, which is usually caused by insufficient sunlight.

CATMINT

Nepeta faassenii (=mussinii)

Origin

Mediterranean area.

Catmint

Uses

Catmint makes an attractive border to a herb garden. It is also a good ground cover and is especially beneficial to roses and lavender. It is an ideal herb for a hanging basket and can also be used to soften the edges of containers. It cuts well for fresh flower arrangements. The leaves can be dried for adding to potpourri. This herb appeals greatly to some cats who partake of it as a medicine (see also CATNIP).

Nepeta faassenii

Height in flower 20 cm (8 in). It has a trailing habit which spreads from clumps of root. Typical stems are square with pairs of toothed, grey leaves. Catmint is low-growing until the stems produce whorls of soft blue/mauve flowers in midsummer. When obtainable there is also a tall variety, Six Hill Giant, which is especially beautiful when it is planted among roses. There is also a smaller-leaved variety of catmint which is very compact.

Cultivation

Catmint is a perennial which can be grown from seed sown in trays. It is usually propagated by root division in the cool season or by cuttings. A sunny position with well-drained, slightly alkaline soil is preferred. After flowering, cut back to basal clump where there is usually a good growth of new leaves.

CATNIP

Nepeta cataria

Origin

Mediterranean area.

Catnip

Nepeta cataria

Height 50 cm (20 in) when in flower. This herb is a perennial. Its typical square stems have toothed, heart-shaped leaves which grow in pairs. The leaves are soft green with greying undersides. The stems branch and the whorls of white flowers have tiny, distinct red spots on the lip of each floret.

Medicinal Uses

N.B. CATNIP is not to be confused with CATMINT. For a warming drink to relieve the misery of a cold, infuse a few catnip leaves with two sage leaves in 250 ml (½ pt) boiling water. To treat bedwetting in a young child, give 125 ml (4 fl oz) of the tea flavoured with honey about two hours before bedtime. A sprig of marjoram may be substituted for the sage. (There is usually an underlying cause behind bedwetting, such as anxiety.) To alleviate bruises, macerate the leaves, warm the resulting pulp and use it as a poultice.

Other uses

Catnip is grown mainly for the pleasure of cats. They eat it when they think medication is required and they also just roll in it for sheer joy. They become completely besotted when rolling in catnip. Dried leaves stuffed into cotton bags provide playthings for cats. To dry, tie in bundles and crumble for use.

Cultivation

Propagate from root division in the autumn. Cuttings take easily and catnip will often self-sow. Plant in a sunny position where the soil should be slightly alkaline and well drained. The plants need a fair amount of water, but good drainage. Cut back plants when growth is lush. If cats start to make plants tatty, cover with wire netting until growth improves.

CELERY

Apium graveolens

Origin

Mediterranean coastal area.

Celery

Culinary Uses

Leaves and stalks are cut from the outside of the plant, chopped and cooked in stews and soups. Celery stalks are cooked with root vegetables like carrots, turnips and so on. Tender, crisp, blanched stalks are eaten in salads and as crudités. Seeds are a flavouring in pickles. Remove the leaves from the stems and dry them on a rack. Finely ground dried seeds combined with salt make a good celery salt. Grind equal parts of dried lemon verbena leaves and celery seed for use in salt-free diets.

Medicinal Uses

Relieve the pain of inflammatory complaints by drinking celery tea. The dosage is 5 ml (1 flat tsp) seed or 15 ml (1 tbsp) chopped leaf and/or stalk, covered with 250 ml (½ pt) boiling water. Allow to stand for at least five minutes. Strain and drink 125 ml (4 fl oz) twice a day. This tea also acts as a sedative.

Cultivation

Celery is a biennial grown from seed sown in situ or in trays in spring and autumn. Celery self-sows freely. Plant it in full sun in rich soil and keep well watered. Harvest some seed as it ripens for later sowing. To blanch celery stems for salad, plant it in trenches and heap soil around the stems as they grow or place cloches over the plants.

Apium graveolens

Height 40 cm (16 in). Celery consists of a cluster of crisp, overlapping, fluted stems, which branch towards the top, bearing pairs of leaves. The leaves are shiny, bright green and deeply indented. Celery bears umbels of creamy green flowers in the second year.

CHAMOMILE

Anthemis nobilis (Roman or lawn chamomile)
Matricaria recutita (German or annual chamomile)

Origin

Europe and areas of Asia.

Roman chamomile

Culinary Uses

The foliage has a fresh, apple-like fragrance. Stir the flowers into sour cream for serving over baked potatoes. Try adding a few flowers to a white sauce or herb butter.

Medicinal Uses

Chamomile is a calming and sleep-inducing herb. Use 10 ml (2 tsps) dried flowers to make a cup of tea. To treat a stye on the eyelid, apply a compress dipped in this solution and repeat as often as possible.

Other Uses

Chamomile leaves and flowers make a refreshing bath and foot bath. To lighten and condition fair hair, make a rinse by simmering 10 ml (2 tsps) dried flowers in 250 ml (1 cup) water for 15–20 minutes. Flowers are dried face down for potpourri. Dried leaves and flowers are added to sleep-pillow stuffing.

Cultivation

Chamomile is usually propagated by root division or from cuttings. Sow the annual variety in situ in the early spring. The soil needs to be sandy and slightly acid and the position sunny, except in hot, dry climates when shading from the midday sun is necessary. Grow chamomile as an edging and allow it to spread through paved paths. The fragrance rises when the plant is walked on and slightly bruised. It is not suitable for areas with heavy traffic. It can be used to soften the edge of a large container of other herbs. For drying, cut the flowers from the stems with scissors and dry them on muslin-covered racks. After flowering, cut the plants back to the main growth. Before putting the annual variety on the compost heap, either shake the seeds into the garden for the following year or save them for sowing.

German chamomile

Anthemis nobilis

It is a perennial ground cover, growing in tufted clumps of fine, feathery foliage with an apple fragrance. Slender stems bear white, daisy-like flowers. The single variety has a prominent yellow boss with down-turned petals. The double variety has a tight head of cream petals.

Matricaria recutita

Height 50 cm (30 in). This herb has an upright growth with fine, feathery foliage. It has branching stems with small, single daisy flowers with a greenish-yellow boss. It is not as highly perfumed as *A. nobilis*, as the flowers smell but the leaves do not.

Chervil

CHERVIL

Anthriscus cerefolium

Origin

Eastern Europe.

Culinary Uses

Chervil has a pleasant, sweet and slightly resinous flavour. It is one of the herbs used to make *fines herbes* and Ravigoti sauce. This delicate herb, which should be snipped with scissors from the outside edge of the plant and then chopped finely, enhances the flavour of chicken, fish, herb butter, cottage cheese, vegetables, salads and all egg dishes. The leaves should always be used fresh, except in *fines herbes* for which they may be dried.

Medicinal Uses

Warm leaves in boiling water and use the resulting pulp as a poultice for the relief of bruising. For a tonic and blood purifier which can be taken twice a day for a fortnight, make chervil tea with two or three sprigs to 250 ml (½ pt) boiling water.

For a facial toner, pour 250 ml (½ pt) boiling water over 60 ml (4 tbsps) chopped leaves and stems. After it has cooled, strain and store the liquid in the fridge. Make a fresh brew every five days.

Anthriscus cerefolium

Height 30–50 cm (12–20 in). Chervil has soft, light green, lacy foliage growing on upright stems. There are umbels of white flowers.

Cultivation

Sow chervil at any time throughout the year (except in very hot areas) in situ or in containers. This herb does not transplant well. For successful germination the seed needs to be fresh. Germination is rapid and takes approximately 7–12 days. The soil needs to be light, composted and well drained. Water the seedlings frequently, especially during hot weather. Chervil prefers to grow in the shelter of larger plants, especially in hot areas, but does not thrive in the drip area of trees.

A fine display of herbs enhances a shady corner of a suburban garden

CHICKWEED

Stellaria media

Origin

Unknown.

Chickweed

Stellaria media

This herb is a low, trailing 'weed'. It has delicate, light green, heart-shaped leaves which grow from branched, slender, brittle stems. It has sparse, starry white flowers.

Culinary Uses

With scissors, cut lush bunches as required. Young stems and leaves are lightly chopped and stirred into egg dishes, soups and stews at the end of cooking time. If used on its own as a vegetable, cook gently in a little butter for a very short while. For salads, strip leaves from the stem and use without chopping.

Medicinal Uses

For a general tonic, steep 60 ml (4 tbsps) chopped leaves and stems in 250 ml (½ pt) boiling water for five minutes. Drink this daily for a fortnight. The same solution may be used to wash septic sores and if strained carefully, it is an excellent eyewash. Chickweed also makes a good poultice when warmed, as the leaves have drawing properties.

Other Uses

Chickweed can also be used as food for caged birds.

Cultivation

Chickweed is an annual which can be found growing in most gardens that are not too well weeded. If there is none in your garden, dig up a clump from a friend's garden and allow to self-sow. Chickweed requires full sun or semi-shade and an average soil which should not be allowed to dry out in summer. It will survive a mild frost.

CHIVES

Allium schoenoprasum (common chive)
A. tuberosum (Chinese or garlic chive)

Origin

Europe, Asia, Siberia and certain regions of Northern America.

Common chives

Culinary Uses

Allium schoenoprasum has an onion flavour and is one of the components of *fines herbes*. *A. tuberosum* is garlic flavoured. This herb is used raw as a garnish and also to flavour salads, herb butters, herb cheeses, stews, egg dishes and soups. Use it to flavour a sandwich with tomato.

Garlic chives

Allium schoenoprasum

Height 25–30 cm (10–12 in). This is a small, onion-like bulb with long, fine roots, growing in clumps. The foliage is in the form of hollow, grey/green, grass-like shoots. Soft, pinky mauve heads of flowers are produced on firm straight stems.

Allium tuberosum

Height 30–35 cm (12–14 in). It consists of loose clumps of small rhizomes with short roots. The foliage is flat, narrow and dark green. Heads of small, starry white flowers grow on stiff upright stems. There are many varieties of *Allium*, both culinary and ornamental.

A. tuberosum is also used freely in Chinese cooking. Vinegars and oils are made using the flowers and foliage. The flowers of the *Allium schoenoprasum* are edible and when separated from the head, make a decorative and tasty garnish.

Other Uses

These are decorative flowers for fresh arrangements. Even when *Allium schoenoprasum* flowers are dried, the colour is good enough to use in arrangements.

Cultivation

Both varieties can be grown from seed sown in trays. They are, however, easier to propagate by dividing clumps into six to eight plants in spring and autumn. It is necessary to do this every two or three years. Grow them in full sun in a good soil enriched with bone meal and used coffee grounds. Chives may be grown in a container. In some areas the plants die back to shoot up again as the weather warms. When harvesting chives, use scissors and cut only half of a clump, leaving about 5 cm (2 in) of growth. This way the plants recover quickly.

Diseases

Rust can attack chives. Cut down to 5 cm (2 in), remove all other foliage and burn. Feed plants well. A copper spray may be applied if the attack is particularly severe.

COMFREY

Symphytum officinale

Origin

Europe and Asia.

Comfrey

Culinary Uses

Although comfrey is a nutritious herb, it should be used sparingly. The young leaves, which have a cucumber flavour, are gently cooked as a vegetable, added fresh to a salad or dipped in batter and fried as fritters. Finely cut leaves are added to stews and soups before serving.

Medicinal Uses

Make a tea of about 5 ml (1 tsp) crushed, dried comfrey to 250 ml (½ pt) boiling water and take this twice a day to alleviate the pains of inflammatory complaints like arthritis and rheumatism and as a general tonic. Comfrey tablets, obtainable from a pharmacy or health shop, taken three times a day, may prove easier as the dosage is better controlled. Comfrey tablets also speed up the healing of broken bones, as does the tea – in fact, the old name for comfrey is knitbone or boneset. The herb contains allantoin which promotes cell development. A poultice of leaves dipped in hot water can be applied to bruises and sprains. To prevent possible skin irritation, first apply a thin layer of Vaseline or comfrey cream over the affected area, then apply the poultice. Comfrey cream or ointment, either home-made (see page 19) or purchased, heals varicose ulcers, nappy rash and other open sores.

Symphytum officinale

Height 70 cm (28 in). There is lush growth from a strong taproot. The dark green leaves are ovate at the base, becoming pointed. The length is approximately 25 cm (10 in), growing in fountain-shaped clumps. These leaves with deep veining are covered with rough bristles which are even thicker on the underside. The flowering stems have small, smoother leaves. Clusters of bell-shaped, mauve flowers droop from one side of each stem.

Other Uses

Feed comfrey to poultry to increase egg production. A small quantity added to dog food improves the skin and coat. The high potash content makes comfrey a good liquid fertilizer (see page 14). Add it to compost heaps as an activator and use surplus foliage as a mulch.

Cultivation

Comfrey is a perennial. Propagate it by root or crown division. Root cuttings may also be struck in spring or autumn. Grow in sun or semi-shade, away from other plants as comfrey spreads easily and can be difficult to remove without damaging its neighbours. The soil should be well-manured and slightly acid. Cut down as flowers begin to form and the plants will then produce new growth rapidly. Comfrey tends to die back in winter. Lift and divide it every two or three years.

CORIANDER

Coriandrum sativum (Chinese parsley or danhia)

Coriander

Coriandrum sativum

Height 50 cm (20 in). The first leaves, known as danhia, are dark green, finely scalloped or round. The secondary leaves are fine, light green and feathery on slender stems. The flowers are umbels of dainty mauve or pink which in turn become clusters of round, green seeds. Leave these until brown and ripe.

Origin

Eastern Mediterranean.

Culinary Uses

The green seeds have a revolting smell so only use them when they have turned pale brown on the plant. They are dried by using the bag treatment (see page 16) and will then have a sweet, pungent flavour and aroma. Roast lightly for an even better flavour. Keep some in a pepper grinder for easy flavouring of cakes, biscuits, breads, gingerbread and some preserves like marmalade and tomato jam. Use in marinades, and also in boerewors and biltong (South African sausage and dried meat). Whole seeds are one of the ingredients in pickling spice and they are also added to herb vinegars and oils. The young, flat leaves can be roughly chopped and added to salads or to curries and stews during the last few minutes of cooking. This is an acquired taste.

Other Uses

Whole, dried seeds mixed in pot-pourri act as a form of fixative for the volatile oils. The pretty flowers cut well for fresh arrangements.

Cultivation

Coriander is an annual grown from seed sown in situ. Germination takes approximately 10 days and sowing is continuous for most of the year. (Do not sow the roasted seed.) Plants need to be in fairly close clumps to support each other. Very small seedlings will transplant. They are suitable for planting in an average-sized container. A well-composted, light soil is required. Do not allow it to dry out in hot weather. For a constant supply of young leaves, nip out the young centre stems to retard the secondary growth. Do not sow coriander near fennel or dill.

American cress

CRESS VARIETIES

Barbarea verna (American cress or landcress)
Lepidium sativum (garden cress)
Nasturtium officinale (watercress)

AMERICAN CRESS

Origin

North America.

Culinary Uses

It has a strong, peppery, mustard flavour. Cut leaves from the outer edge of the plant. Use sparingly in salads, sandwiches, herb butters, cottage cheese and sauces. Cut or tear the leaves – do not chop.

Barbarea verna

Height 15 cm (6 in). It is taller when in flower. It grows close to the ground in the form of a rosette with short-stemmed, shiny green, lobed leaves. In the second year, the tall stems are topped with heads of bright yellow flowers.

Cultivation

Propagate from seed throughout the year. American cress self-sows well if seed is allowed to set. If no commercial seed is available, buy a plant and allow seed to set for sowing or allow to self-sow. Seedlings will transplant. This herb is suitable for containers. American cress requires a rich soil, occasionally mulched with well-rotted manure. It will grow in sun or semi-shade. The plants provide good eating for two years, then the leaves tend to become bitter. American cress is frost-sensitive.

Garden cress

GARDEN CRESS

Origin

Middle East.

Culinary Uses

Snip with scissors for sandwiches, salads, egg dishes and garnishing.

Cultivation

Garden cress is an annual. It is usually sown with mustard seed in a tray of fine soil. Sow seed thickly

Lepidium sativum

Height 5–8 cm (2–3 in). Delicate plants have fine, light green leaves.

Watercress

Nasturtium officinale

This herb is a water-loving plant. Trailing growth sends down white roots from the stems. Dark green, shiny, round to pinnate leaves grow in sprigs from these stems. The small flowers are white.

and keep damp. Germination takes approximately seven days. If it is grown indoors, make sure there is plenty of light. It can be grown in rows in situ but needs to be shaded until ready to be cut. Sow garden cress continuously throughout the year. When the plants are 5–8 cm (2–3 in) high, cut down as required.

WATERCRESS

Origin

Western and Central Europe.

Culinary Uses

Watercress has a tangy, peppery flavour. It is used as a garnish and is also good in sandwiches and salads. Make it into a purée or use leaves whole in a sauce. This is especially good with fish. Watercress soup may be served either hot or cold. For the best flavour, pick watercress before the flowers appear.

Cultivation

Propagate by sowing seed in trays or, easier still, from rooting stems. A few sprigs from a bunch bought at the market will soon produce roots if left in water. Transplant to containers to be sunk in a pond or a gently flowing stream. The pond will need to be aerated once a week by running in fresh water. Watercress will also grow in a very damp corner of the garden. *N.B. Unless at the source of a stream, it is inadvisable to harvest from streams or canals because of possible contamination by chemicals, animals or humans.*

CURRY BUSH

Helichrysum petiolare (=angustifolium)

Origin

Southern Africa.

Curry bush

Culinary Uses

This herb has a curry flavour and aroma. Tender tips or sprigs added to a curry enhance the flavour without adding to the strength of the

Helichrysum petiolare

Height 45 cm (17 in). It is a sub-shrub, indigenous to Southern Africa. The pinnate, silver green leaves grow from firm, downy, grey/white stems. The heads are small, ochre/yellow flowers.

spices. Remove before serving. Stir finely chopped young foliage into mayonnaise, salad dressing, soups or stews. Scatter over vegetables and egg dishes. An easy way to prepare a small quantity of leaves is to put them in a cup and snip with scissors until fine. The flowers may be added to pickles and vinegars.

Other Uses

Cut stems of flowers, tie them in a bunch and hang them up to dry for potpourri. Curry bush gives an attractive, silver foliage accent in a border or garden bed.

Cultivation

Propagate curry bush from small heel cuttings in spring and autumn. This plant is not fussy about soil but needs a sunny, well-drained position. Prune it back after flowering otherwise the plant becomes very woody. Curry bush makes a neat, low hedge and has an average life span of four years. It is also suitable for planting in a container.

DANDELION

Taraxacum officinale

Origin

Northern Europe.

Dandelion

Culinary Uses

It has a bland, slightly bitter flavour. Because of their high vitamin and mineral content, the young leaves from the centre of the plant are excellent as salad greens. Before cooking the more mature outer leaves, soak them in salt water for half an hour to remove bitterness, then rinse well. Do not take too many leaves from one plant. Cut buds with stalks, then discard stalks. Collect 60 ml (4 tbsps) dandelion buds, fry gently in a little butter and add this to a two-egg omelette or scrambled egg. Mature roots can be lifted, scrubbed, minced, dried and roasted, then used in the same way as a chicory mixture or simply as a coffee substitute.

Taraxacum officinale

Dandelion has a rosette of leaves close to the ground, growing from deep, fleshy roots. It has bright green, deeply scalloped leaves. A hollow, upright stem bears a bright yellow, flattened, daisy-like flower with downward-turning green bracts. *N.B. This herb is not to be confused with a tough weed with a similar flower which inhabits lawns.*

Medicinal Uses

As a general tonic, simmer 30 g (1 oz) dried root in 500 ml (1 pt) water for approximately 10 minutes (do not boil). Strain and store the liquid in the fridge. The dose is one sherry glassful a day. This infusion also acts as a mild diuretic. To treat warts, apply the milk from the stems several times a day.

Cultivation

Dandelion is a perennial which self-sows readily. The young seedlings can easily be transplanted. To control seeding, remove mature flowers. Dandelion grows lushly in rich, composted soil. Water well, especially in hot weather. Surplus plants may be chopped for composting.

DILL

Anethum graveolens

Origin

Unknown.

Dill

Culinary Uses

The mild, spicy leaves of this herb taste of caraway while the seeds are strongly pungent and aromatic. Freshly cut and lightly chopped leaves enhance the flavour of dips, cottage cheese, herb butters, soups, salads and all fish dishes. When the seeds are pale brown, dry them using the bag method (see page 16). Dill seeds are commonly used in pickled cucumber and cabbage and they also improve the taste of roasts, stews, cooked vegetables and potato and cucumber salads. They are good sprinkled on breads, rolls and fruit pies. Grind the seeds and use as a salt substitute in the diet. Take the flowering heads as well as seeds to make dill vinegar (see page 17).

Medicinal Uses

To relieve indigestion, steep approximately 5 ml (1 tsp) dill seed in 250 ml (½ pt) boiling water. When cold, strain and refrigerate until needed. The adult dosage is 15 ml (1 tbsp) as required. Use less for children according to their age. The above mixture diluted with 60 ml (2 fl oz) water and taken during the course of the day helps to increase lactation in a nursing mother.

Anethum graveolens

Height 60 cm (24 in). A hollow, upright main stem grows from a long taproot. Dill has loose, feathery, blue/green leaves with umbels of fine, yellow flowers. The flat, oval seeds are pale brown with a dark rib down the centre.

Cultivation

Dill is an annual. Sow in situ as seedlings do not transplant well. Cover the seeds lightly – germination takes one to two weeks. Sow continuously except in the coldest season. Allow to grow in fairly close clumps for support, in sun or semi-shade where the soil is well-drained, light and slightly acid. Do not grow near caraway, fennel or angelica.

Pests

Caterpillars (see page 11).

ELDER

Sambucus nigra
S. nigra argentea 'Variegata'
(cream and green elder)
S. nigra aurea (gold elder)

Origin

Europe, North America and Asia.

Elder

Culinary Uses

The flowers have a soft, sweet taste while the berries are slightly sour. For a simple dessert, dip flower heads in a light batter, deep-fry until just golden, drain on paper, remove main stem and sift with castor sugar. To flavour buns, scones and breads, place flower heads in a plastic bag and leave in the sun for an hour to sweat. Florets are then easily removed from the stems, ready to be added to dough mixtures. Cut sprays of berries when they turn purple – they are a good addition to apple in a pie or tart. Stew with any other available fruit. A very palatable jelly is made from the berries, as is sambuca, an interesting liqueur.

Medicinal Uses

For serious problems, this herb should be taken under supervision. For a hangover, try an elder and yarrow tea. The discomfort of a cold can be relieved by sipping, when needed, a tea of about 5 ml (1 tsp) chopped elder leaves, 2.5 ml (½ tsp) chopped peppermint and a pinch of cayenne. A soothing cough syrup is made by crushing the berries, then straining and mixing the juice with honey. Keep refrigerated to prevent fermentation. A poultice of leaves warmed in hot water is a treatment for bruises and sprains.

Other Uses

To make a facial tonic, steep 30 ml (2 heaped tbsps) fresh flowers in 250 ml (½ pt) boiling water. Strain when cold. Keep refrigerated. Pat on face after cleansing. Make larger quantities if needed as a face-wash for an acne condition.

Cultivation

Propagate elder from 25 cm (10 in) hardwood cuttings in autumn. Mature trees produce suckers which can be removed and transplanted. Self-sown saplings may also be found nearby. Elder is not fussy about growing conditions. It may be pruned to a required shape, for example a tall hedge.

FENNEL

Foeniculum vulgare
(common fennel)
F. purpurascens (bronze fennel)
F. vulgare var. *dulce*
(Florentine fennel)

Origin

Mediterranean. Fennel has also been known to the Chinese, Indians and Egyptians since ancient times.

Culinary Uses

F. vulgare and *F. purpurascens*
These have a warm, sweet, aniseed flavour. Young leaves are cooked as a vegetable. Add chopped foliage to meat, chicken and fish. Wrap a whole fish in fennel leaves before placing on barbecue coals. Flavour butters, cheeses, mayonnaise, oils, vinegars, salads and egg dishes with young leaves. Allow seeds to become almost dry, then remove heads and give them the bag treatment (see page 16). Crushed or whole, fennel seeds are used to add flavour to breads, rolls, butters, cheeses, sauces and fish dishes.

F. vulgare var. *dulce*
When the bulb-like, swollen stem has reached the size of a tennis ball, remove the outer covering, wash

Sambucus nigra

Height 4 m (20 ft). The elder is a deciduous, bushy tree. It has woody stems with oval, serrated, matt green, loose leaves and masses of flat-topped umbels of creamy white, star-shaped, fragrant flowers. Later the branches tend to droop with the weight of small purple/black berries. A cold spell in autumn produces even more berries than usual.

Common fennel

Bronze fennel

Foeniculum vulgare

May reach 3 m (10 ft). It has a thick, perennial rootstock producing strong, erect, cylindrical, smooth, bright green stems. Many branches grow from the sheaths on the stems. The sprays of feathery foliage are a lush green when young, later maturing to a dull green. There are flat umbels of bright yellow flowers. The greenish-brown seeds are curved and ribbed.

Foeniculum purpurascens

This herb only grows to about 1 m (3½ ft) and has distinct bronze foliage. The flowers are golden.

Foeniculum vulgare var. *dulce*

Height 75 cm (2¼ ft). The stalks are pale green and the umbels of yellow flowers are loose. This variety is grown especially for its bulb-like, swollen stem, delicious in a salad.

well, cook lightly and serve with a cheese sauce. Alternatively, slice it thinly and use it raw as a salad with a vinaigrette dressing.

Florentine fennel

Medicinal Uses

To relieve constipation and aid digestion, add 15 ml (1 tbsp) freshly chopped leaves or 5 ml (1 tsp) seeds to 250 ml (½ pt) boiling water. For children, give small doses according to age. Strained carefully, this solution is used as an eyewash. The foliage and seeds of *F. purpurascens* and *F. vulgare* var. *dulce* may also be used like those of *F. vulgare*.

Cultivation

Fennel is propagated from seed sown in situ as the seedlings do not transplant very well. It self-sows generously. Remove any unwanted seedlings while they are still young. Owing to a long, sturdy taproot, mature plants do not uproot easily. Fennel grows in most soils and positions but the richer the soil the more tender the foliage. None of the fennel varieties should be planted next to either dill or coriander. *F. vulgare* var. *dulce* is grown from seed and is treated as an annual, because the plant is lifted when the 'bulb' is mature. To promote bulb growth and to blanch, heap soil around the stem. Good soil, a sunny position and adequate watering is necessary. Remove flowering heads not wanted for seed to promote bulb growth.

FEVERFEW

Tanacetum parthenium
(=*Chrysanthemum parthenium*)

Origin

Asia Minor, Britain and Europe.

Feverfew

Medicinal Uses

Feverfew has an aromatic, bittersweet fragrance. It is used in the treatment of inflammatory conditions and migraine. There is no instant cure for migraine but over a period of time, as feverfew builds up in the body, the attacks should diminish. *N.B. It should be taken under supervision or bought in pill or capsule form from a pharmacy to ensure that the dosage is controlled.*

Other Uses

It attracts aphids away from roses and other plants. It is an attractive garden plant and a long-lasting cut flower. The flowers are dried face down for potpourri.

Cultivation

Feverfew is a perennial which self-sows readily so there are usually new plants coming up in the garden. If sowing seed, do so in spring. Propagate the double variety with cuttings in spring and autumn. Grow feverfew in full sun in average soil. Cut back to basal growth at the end of the flowering time.

Pests and Diseases

Aphids and, if planted in the shade, mildew (see page 11).

HOREHOUND

Marrubium vulgare (white horehound)

Origin

Europe.

Culinary Uses

Horehound has a bitter taste. Use only small quantities to season meat.

Medicinal Uses

Cut sprigs of young flowers and leaves to make a tea which loosens phlegm, eases a cough and 'wheezing of lungs' (to quote Culpepper). The proportions for this tea are four or five chopped leaves to 250 ml (½ pt) boiling water. Honey and lemon may be added to improve the flavour. This tea also helps to relieve a feverish cold. One cupful should be taken in the course of the day.

Horehound

Tanacetum parthenium

Height 50 cm (20 in). Sturdy, upright, branching stalks bear loose clusters of small, single white daisies with bright yellow, flat centres. Fern-like, bright green leaves are much divided. There is a double-flowered variety and also a very pretty single-flowered, golden-foliaged feverfew.

Marrubium vulgare

Height 40 cm (16 in). It has an upright growth of square, furry stalks with a pair of crumpled leaves at each joint. The oval leaves are soft and grey/green. Whorls of small white flowers cluster around the joints. The flowers turn into seeds which are contained in prickly husks. The leaves have a pleasant aroma when they are crushed.

Overuse causes diarrhoea. A simple herb candy relieves coughs and eases a sore throat (see page 19).

Cultivation

The seed is slow to germinate so cuttings and root division are more satisfactory ways of propagation. (In Australia horehound is categorised as a noxious weed.) It will self-sow but I prefer to remove most flowers before the seed sets – the husks are a nuisance as they stick to clothing and are difficult to remove. Keep the plant trimmed to prevent it from straggling as it matures.

HORSERADISH

Armoracia rusticana

Origin

Southeastern Europe and western regions of Asia.

Horseradish

Culinary Uses

This is a bitingly pungent herb. Horseradish contains a highly volatile oil which evaporates readily, therefore it is not cooked. The root is scrubbed and grated or processed as quickly as possible as one is apt to weep from the fumes. If using a grater, take it outside. Combine the horseradish with cream and chopped nuts to make a good sauce with many uses. This herb may also be added to butters, cottage cheese, white sauce, yoghurt and salad dressings. To make a pickle, combine 1 part grated root with 2 parts vinegar and a little salt. Grated raw beetroot is often added to this. Very young leaves, cut from close to the base, are used in salads.

Medicinal Uses

Taken regularly, horseradish is an effective tonic and digestive. To treat stings and insect bites, squash leaves in a little boiling water, allow to cool and dab on afflicted area frequently.

Armoracia rusticana

Height 60cm (24 in). Horseradish has a deep, thick, white taproot with smaller branching roots growing out at an angle. Large, dark green leaves grow from the root stem, somewhat like coarse, pointed spinach leaves. As the plant matures, serrated or deeply lobed leaves appear. The leaves have a characteristic smell when they are crushed.

Cultivation

Horseradish is a perennial. It is usually propagated from thick root cuttings of 12 cm (4½ in) in length or when a main root is dug up. A 5 cm (2 in) piece is cut off the top of the root with a little of the greenery and planted in a sunny position in a light, well-manured soil to which some bone meal has been added. Keep it well watered. In some areas plants tend to die back in winter. Cut the flowering stem as soon as it appears. Do not try to harvest the seed as it is usually infertile.

Pests

Slugs and snails (see page 12).

LAVENDER

As there are over fifty listed varieties, I will deal here only with the most common:

Lavandula angustifolia
(English lavender)
L. dentata (French lavender)
L. dentata var. *candicans*
(French lavender)

Origin

Mediterranean region, Asia Minor, India and Atlantic islands.

English lavender

Lavender

French lavender

Culinary Uses

Lavender has a strong, spicy flavour. When making apple jelly, mix in six flower heads to each litre (2 pt) of juice. Remove before bottling. To improve the flavour of indifferent honey, stir in a few flowers and allow to stand. To make an old Elizabethan cake icing, crush sufficient lavender flowers into the icing sugar for a good colour and then stir in a little rose-water and lemon or orange juice for the correct consistency. A few flower heads may be broken up and added to a salad for colour and flavour. Try cooking chicken with a few sprigs of fresh lavender instead of rosemary.

Medicinal Uses

Lavender oil obtained from a pharmacy is rubbed on the temples to assist sleep and soothe away a headache. For bruises, sprains, aching muscles and joints, blend lavender oil with rosemary oil and arnica (obtainable from pharmacies). For an antiseptic rinse, pour 500 ml (1 pt) boiling water over 60 ml (4 tbsps) broken flower heads and a few leaves. Strain and use the liquid when cold. Insomnia sufferers find a tea made with four or five flower heads to 250 ml (½ pt) boiling water, taken with a little honey, is sleep-inducing. Make it in a small Thermos flask so as to be able to sip it on becoming wakeful in the middle of the night. A lavender pillow is also sleep-inducing. It is said that a sprig of lavender worn under one's hat will prevent or cure a headache.

Other Uses

A lavender bath is relaxing. After pruning, bunch and hang foliage to dry for potpourri and for its anti-moth properties. Lavender is an attractive garden plant and a useful cut flower. Cut flowers on a full length of stem when almost completely open. Place a few broken up stems and foliage in the bag of the vacuum cleaner to scent the house. To dry the flowers, cut them as soon as they begin to open.

Cultivation

Lavenders are grown from seed sown in trays. This is done when varieties are not available to take cuttings. Propagating from small heel or tip cuttings is more usual. A sunny, well-drained position with slightly alkaline soil is required. The

French lavender (candicans)

Lavandula angustifolia

Height 1.5 m (5 ft). This variety is a subshrub. Strong, grey stems branch out near ground level. These stems become woody with maturity. The many small branches have narrow, downy, blue/grey leaves, slightly serrated. Stiff, elongated stems bear compact circles of small lavender-coloured flowers for about 10 cm (4 in) from the tip.

Lavandula dentata var. *candicans*

Height 80 cm (32 in). The growth is slightly woody. The leaves are grey and serrated. Stems of about 20 cm (8 in) long have fat cones of dense lavender-coloured flowers.

Lavandula dentata

Height 70 cm (28 in). This variety is a compact subshrub with small, green, serrated leaves. Short slender stems bear cone-shaped clusters of blue/grey flowers.

addition of a little agricultural lime and bone meal is advisable when planting. Cut bushes back hard after flowering to keep compact and to encourage further flowering. Lavenders can be clipped into low, compact hedges for edging beds and are useful in a formal herb garden. With the exception of tall varieties like *Lavandula angustifolia*, these small shrubs can be grown in containers of a suitable size. Some other varieties which might be found by diligent searching are dwarf and average-sized *stoechas* (Spanish/Italian), dwarf Munstead, Hidcote, Folgate Blue and grey and green varieties of fern-leaved lavender.

Pests and Diseases

Australian bug (see page 11) and also yellowing of foliage, usually caused by poor drainage.

LEMON BALM

Melissa officinalis

Origin

Mountains of southern Europe.

Lemon balm

Culinary Uses

This herb has a lemon flavour and fragrance. Add a few torn young leaves to a salad. Leaves of lemon balm may be used to flavour milk puddings, custards and quiches. Chopped leaves enhance chicken and fish dishes – they are best added in the last few minutes of cooking time. They may also be sprinkled over cooked vegetables.

Medicinal Uses

Apply crushed leaves to insect bites. Lemon balm makes a most refreshing tea which is a calmative tonic, helps to bring down a fever and also combats heat exhaustion. Use about six to eight leaves in 250 ml (½ pt) boiling water.

Other Uses

Make a stronger brew of the tea as a rinse for greasy hair. As a facial steam, lemon balm is said to delay the ageing process. Dry the herb for potpourri. Apiarists rub the insides of new hives with lemon balm in order to settle the bees.

Cultivation

The seed is slow to germinate. It self-sows occasionally. It is usually propagated by root division or by tip cuttings put to root in water. This herb is a root spreader, though not as invasive as mint. After flowering, cut down to where new growth shows above the ground. It requires a well-composted, moist soil in a sunny or semi-shaded position. Protect from midday sun in very hot areas and from frost in winter. It is suitable for growing in a container.

Pests and Diseases

Caterpillars and rust (see page 11).

Melissa officinalis

Height 40 cm (16 in). Lemon balm is a bushy perennial, somewhat similar to mint. The stems are square and brittle and they bear pairs of bright green, crinkly, toothed leaves and small, white flowers.

Herbs and hedges provide a focal point in a country garden

LEMON GRASS

Cymbopogon citratus

Origin

The East.

Lemon grass

Culinary Uses

Lemon grass has a distinct lemon fragrance and flavour when bruised. Young leaves are cut where they fold around the stem. If plants form clusters, both leaves and stems may be cut. Keep them whole to cook with rice, custards, milk puddings, stews and soups and steam with vegetables. Lemon grass enhances fish, chicken, curries and pork. Remove the leaves before serving. In the East, where the leaves are very tender, they are chopped and left in the food. If there is an abundance, the stolons may be dug up, washed, scraped and pounded for cooking like the leaves. Lemon grass also makes a refreshing tea with mint or any other fragrant herb.

Medicinal Uses

Make a weak tea of chopped leaves and drink it to alleviate nausea.

Other Uses

Lemon grass makes a refreshing bath herb. To dry the foliage for pot-pourri, snip it into pieces before spreading on muslin-covered racks.

Cultivation

Propagate lemon grass by lifting and dividing clumps of stolons. Cut the tops off the old growth, leaving approximately 30 cm (12 in). When planting out, make sure the roots are anchored firmly in the ground with part of the stolon just visible above the soil. The soil should be rich and damp. Grow this herb in full sun or semi-shade. As stolons tend to form crowded clumps, it is advisable to divide them every two or three years. Cut back the old foliage when it becomes tatty.

Cymbopogon citratus

Height 1 m (3 ft) in good conditions. It is a tender grass. Bright green foliage forms a tubular sheath around the stem. The foliage is blade-like with a deep centre vein. It tends to bend over on itself. A wiry root system grows from a stolon (which resembes a rough tuber).

LEMON VERBENA

Aloysia triphylla (=Lippia citriodora)

Origin

Chile, Argentina and Mexico.

Lemon Verbena

Culinary Uses

This herb has a strong lemon fragrance and flavour. Finely chopped young leaves may be added to any dish where a lemon flavour is indicated. Sprinkle on fruit or vegetable salad and stir finely chopped leaves into herb butter and cottage cheese. Lemon verbena makes a refreshing tea when made with mint, other herbs or on its own. It is ideal served cold on a hot summer's day. For a reduced salt diet, crush dried leaves and mix in the proportion of one part salt to three parts lemon verbena. It also combines well with dried celery and lovage leaves to make a salt-free seasoning.

Medicinal Uses

Make a tea of six to eight leaves to 250 ml (½ pt) boiling water and use as a digestive or sedative.

Other Uses

It is ideal for potpourri as the dried leaves retain their oils for two or three years if treated correctly. Take branches of leaves throughout the growing season and hang to dry. Cut the mature flowers for fresh indoor arrangements. Place a handful of the leaves in the bag of your vacuum cleaner to scent the house.

Cultivation

Propagate from pencil-sized cuttings, heeled if possible, taken any time except mid-winter. They need protection from frost, so plant them in a sheltered area, though I prefer to plant them near a door or path, as the fragrance is strong when you brush by. Full sun with an average alkaline soil is required. Prune back hard in autumn. Save all leaves for drying so as to have a supply until new leaves appear. The shrub does not stay bare for long.

Pests

Red spider and, when conditions are dry, stink bugs (see page 12).

LETTUCE

Lactuca sativa

Origin

Europe and Britain.

Lettuce

Culinary Uses

Lettuce must be fresh, preferably from garden to table. For salads, tear the leaves for easier eating or leave whole. Do not cut or chop as this causes bruising and discolouration. Cook the more mature leaves in

Aloysia triphylla

Height 60 cm – 1.2 m (2–4 ft). In fact, in hot climates the plant can reach an astonishing 4.5 m (15 ft). It is a shrub with a slender, woody trunk and branches. It has tender stems of light green, thin, lance-shaped, pointed leaves. The leaves are slightly sticky, shiny on top and dull on the undersides. Small pale mauve flowers grow in spikes from summer to autumn.

Lactuca sativa

A wide choice of lettuces is available, among which the 'plucking' varieties are the most interesting. These loose-leaved lettuces do not have heads. The outer leaves are plucked as they are required and the plants continue to grow for months, depending on climatic conditions. Nip out the centres occasionally to prolong growth. They will eventually bolt and self-sow. The most strongly flavoured variety is Mustard Lettuce, which has large, bright green leaves with frilled, serrated edges. The leaves of some other varieties like Australian Yellow, American Brown, Oak Leaf, Lollo Rosso, Red Salad Bowl, Rubin and Round Leaf vary in colour from lime green to deep red. Some are deeply indented, while others have frilly edges.

chicken stock as a good summer soup. Steam young peas with a sprig of mint in a pot lined with mature lettuce leaves and very little water. Braise lettuce leaves to serve as a vegetable. Dry the seed of Mustard Lettuce by using the bag method (see page 16). It is a good substitute for true mustard as a seasoning.

Medicinal Uses

Lettuce should be included in the diet, especially for its mild laxative properties. Nursing mothers find that a daily helping of lettuce will help to improve lactation. There are also proprietary cough syrups and pills for insomnia which are made from lettuce concentrates. It is also rich in vitamin E – the fertility vitamin. (Rabbits eat lettuce!)

Other Uses

Lettuce is used for colour in the garden. It makes an excellent border plant, especially the more colourful varieties (see page 49).

Cultivation

Lettuces are annuals. Propagate them by sowing seed in trays throughout the year. Seeds may also be sown in situ and seedlings thinned and transplanted at the four-leaf stage. Mustard Lettuce and loose-leaved varieties self-sow readily. In hot weather, plant in semi-shade or protect from the midday sun. A light, well-drained and composted soil is required. Keep plants well watered. When plants bolt and go to seed, leave seed to mature on the plants, then lift, shake the seed over the ground and cover lightly. Nurseries often have punnets with two or three varieties of loose-leaved lettuce which are sufficient for the needs of one or two people. They are suitable for growing in containers.

Pests

Slugs and snails (see page 12).

LOVAGE

Levisticum officinale

Origin

Southern Europe and the Balkans.

Lovage

Culinary Uses

Lovage has a strong, spicy flavour, almost like a cross between celery and parsley. It is known as 'Maggi' on the European continent. Care should be taken not to damage the centre growth when cutting the foliage. Chop young leaves finely and add to salads – it is strong, so use it sparingly. When the stems are cooked as a vegetable, first remove leaves for drying. Dried powdered root, leaves and crushed seeds are used to flavour soups and stews. Stems and foliage may take up to four weeks to dry, depending on weather conditions. Cut seed heads on stalks and use the paper bag treatment (see page 16). The roots are dug up when the plant is three or four years old and these may be scrubbed, peeled and pickled.

Medicinal Uses

A weak tea made from the root, stem or leaves aids digestion and also acts as a diuretic. ***N.B. Not to be taken during pregnancy or by anyone with a kidney complaint.***

Other Uses

Cut the foliage and use it in fresh decorative arrangements.

Cultivation

Lovage is usually grown from seed sown in trays in spring and autumn. Transplant seedlings into bags when four to six leaves appear. Plant out when well grown. If no commercial seed is available, buy one plant and collect seed from it in due course. It requires well-dug, rich soil in semi-shade. When watering make sure the moisture penetrates well so as to encourage deep rooting. Plants die back in winter. In areas of frost, protect roots with a heavy mulch.

Pests

Aphids, caterpillars, slugs and snails (see page 11).

Levisticum officinale

Average height 1 m (3 ft). A fleshy, carrot-like root produces many straight, brittle, hollow stems. The leaves are flat, leathery, serrated and bright green with small sulphur-yellow flowers which appear in the form of umbels. The seeds are ridged and crescent-shaped.

Nasturtiums add a splash of bright colour to any garden

MARIGOLD

Tagetes patula (French marigold)
T. erecta (African marigold)
T. minuta (Inca marigold, khaki weed)

Origin

Mexico.

African marigold

Uses

Marigold has a pungent aroma. It is an essential plant for healthy soil, especially *T. minuta* (khaki weed). The Incas and other South American Indians planted this herb to keep their limited – usually terraced – growing areas healthy for over a thousand years. Marigolds planted in the garden repel eelworm (nematode) which attacks the root system of potatoes, dahlias, proteas and many other plants. A brew of leaves and soapy water makes a good spray to counteract thrips. For potpourri, use dried flowers and foliage stripped from stems. The seed of khaki weed helps to retain the fragrant oils in potpourri. All three varieties have moth-repellent properties when dried. Both *Tagetes patula* and *T. erecta* brighten a garden and make good cut flowers.

Tagetes patula (French marigold)

Height differs with each variety from 10 cm (4 in) to 2 m (6½ ft) in the case of Inca marigold. Brittle stems branch from an erect, hollow main stalk. The foliage is fairly dense and made up of finely divided leaves, feathery in some instances. The dark green leaves are a foil for the bright single or double yellow and orange flowers. There are also some bi-coloured varieties. Inca marigold (khaki weed) stands erect with sparse branches of fine, dull green, deeply indented leaves and spikes of small, creamy yellow flowers. The seeds are 2 cm (½ in), black at one end and white at the other.

Cultivation

Marigold is usually regarded as a summer-flowering annual. Sow seeds in situ or in trays. It often self-sows and requires average soil in a sunny position. It may be successfully thinned and transplanted. Inca marigold (khaki weed) tends to droop when moved so water the foliage well. Nip out the centres of young plants to provide more stems. Remove dead heads often to prolong flowering. Marigolds are suitable for container planting with the exception of khaki weed and other tall varieties. Be careful when collecting the seed of khaki weed as it sticks to clothing and is difficult to remove.

Pests

Slugs and snails (see page 12).

MINT

Of the many varieties, some of the most used are:
Mentha rotundifolia (crinkle-leaved spearmint)
M. spicata (spearmint)
M. suaveolens (apple mint)
M. piperita (peppermint)
M. pulegium (pennyroyal)

Origin

Southern Europe, the East and many other lands.

Crinkle-leaved spearmint

Mint

Spearmint

Peppermint

Pennyroyal

Apple mint

Culinary Uses

Spearmint and crinkle-leaved spearmint are the best varieties to use for a classic mint sauce (see page 17). Cook mint with peas and young potatoes in order to enhance their flavour. A few leaf tips may be chopped and stirred into butters and cottage cheese. Spearmint makes a most attractive addition to drinks or fruit dishes and is used as a garnish. It also makes a refreshing tea. Make a tea of apple mint, add the leaves to drinks or chop the young leaves to add to a fruit salad. Peppermint makes an excellent flavouring for ice cream, as well as for chocolate desserts and cakes, biscuits, drinks and teas. ***N.B. Pennyroyal should never be taken internally***.

Medicinal Uses

A tea made from any pleasant mint (*except pennyroyal*) acts as a digestive and relieves the discomfort of a cold. Peppermint is very good as a decongestant, particularly of the sinus cavities. Pour boiling water over a few sprigs in a small bowl, place the bowl in a paper bag, then gather the opening of the bag over the nose and mouth and inhale as much as possible for as long as is comfortable. Crushed leaves on the pillow at night are also comforting.

Other Uses

Rub pennyroyal on neck, face and hands to deter insects. It can also be rubbed on a dog's coat and sprigs can be placed in the kennel or basket as a flea deterrent. Plant under roses to retain soil moisture and to keep roses healthier. Allow to grow in walkways for fragrance. Dry any pleasantly fragrant mint, with or without flowers, for potpourri. Mints are good as cut flowers and provide foliage for indoor arrangements.

Cultivation

Propagate mint by root division or cuttings rooted in water. Rooted runners are invasive so plants should be grown in containers or be confined by plastic or other material barriers, buried in the ground in a damp, shady position with rich soil. There are varieties which will take full sun. Cut right down after flowering. Some varieties die back in winter. Mulch against frost damage. Apart from container planting, pennyroyal is a good addition to a hanging basket.

Height varies. All varieties of mint have square stems and pairs of leaves with pungent oil ducts on the undersides. The flowers grow in whorls on stems which vary in length.

Mentha rotundifolia

The leaves are rounded and crinkled and the flowers are blue/mauve.

Mentha spicata

The leaves are long and lightly veined. The flowers are white.

Mentha suaveolens

The leaves are round and furry. There is also a variegated kind with creamy splotches. The flowers are white.

Mentha piperita

The leaves are dark green on purple-tinged stalks. The flowers are mauve.

Mentha pulegium

The leaves are small, shiny and slightly rounded. It is low-growing until the blue/mauve flowers appear.

When mint roots become too dense, lift, divide and replant them or put into pots. Try to locate the many other interesting varieties which your local nurseries or your fellow herb growers may have collected.

Pests and Diseases

Caterpillars and rust (see page 11).

NASTURTIUM
Tropaeolum majus

Origin

South America and Mexico.

Nasturtium

Culinary Uses

It has a strong, pepper/mustard flavour. Nasturtium leaves make an interesting cream soup, garnished with a few flower petals. Tear the leaves and flowers for sandwiches. In a salad, tear the leaves but leave the flowers whole. A small quantity of finely shredded leaves may also be added to a herb butter or cheese dip. Use immediately as the flavour tends to become bitter when stored. A few pulverised green seeds add piquancy to a mayonnaise or salad dressing. Young, green seeds and buds can be pickled for use as a caper substitute (see page 16). Flowers with a 'dollop' of cottage cheese in the centre make a quick, colourful party snack. Stems, leaves, flowers and seeds are used to make nasturtium vinegar (see page 17).

Tropaeolum majus

Nasturtium is a brittle-stemmed plant of sprawling or climbing habit. The stiff, upright stems bear shield-shaped leaves which tend to face upwards. Single or double trumpet-shaped flowers range from creamy yellow and orange to deep red. Flowers have a single nectar-bearing spur at the back. The seeds are large and are formed in three grooved sections. There are also compact dwarf varieties as well as the Whirly Bird variety, which has spurless flowers facing upwards and a more restrained growth habit.

Medicinal Uses

As nasturtium leaves are a natural antibiotic, use them to cure a sore throat. Chew three or four leaves, then another two or three an hour later and repeat if necessary. Do not overdo this treatment. Small children will find the leaves too strong to chew on their own so offer them the leaves on a cracker or a thin slice of bread and butter instead; however, this is not as effective.

Other Uses

Allow plants to grow around fruit trees as they will keep the trees healthier. Dry the flowers face downward for potpourri colour. A bowl of cut flowers brightens any room. To keep the display simple, set the nasturtiums with a few sprigs of their own foliage.

Cultivation

Nasturtiums are usually annual, although there are some perennial varieties available. Perennials are usually propagated from cuttings or from seed. Annuals are grown from seed sown in situ or in containers. The dwarf varieties are the most suitable for containers. Seeds are usually sown in winter but once they have grown in a garden, they self-sow readily. Full sun and average soil are the best conditions for growing nasturtiums. If the soil is too rich there will be more leaves than flowers. Nasturtiums are frost-sensitive.

Pests

Slugs and snails (see page 12).

NETTLE

Urtica dioica

Origin

Europe and Great Britain.

Nettle

Culinary Uses

Cut the young tips before the flower tassels appear and the texture of the leaves becomes gritty. Cook gently to eat as a vegetable, make a creamy nettle soup or serve as spinach, topped with a poached egg. The heat renders the stinging acid in the leaves and stems harmless.

Medicinal Uses

If drying nettle for tea, cut mature stems before the flowers appear. Drink one cup of nettle tea twice a day to alleviate the misery of pollen- or dust-induced hay fever. To make the tea, pour 250 ml (½ pt) boiling water over 5 ml (1 tsp) crushed, dried nettle leaves or six large, fresh leaves. Allow the tea to stand for about five minutes. Strain and add a little honey and lemon if desired. Dried nettle tea is available at pharmacies and health shops.

Other Uses

Young leaves are used to make an astringent facial steam. As a hair rinse, pour 2 parts boiling water

Urtica dioica

Height 1 m (3 ft). A matted network of spreading roots produces stiff, upright stems. The dark green, heart-shaped leaves are toothed and tapered to a point. Flowers on the female plant are in the form of green catkins that appear from early summer to autumn. The downy leaves and stems are covered with tiny sacs of acid which cause blistering of the skin. To soothe, dab the affected area with nettle juice, dock leaves (sorrel) or bulbine.

over 1 part chopped nettle. Allow to cool, strain and keep in the fridge until required. As a herbal compost activator, nettle is unsurpassed.

Cultivation

This herb is a perennial, propagated by root division in spring or by cuttings rooted in water. It is at its best when grown in dampish soil in semi-shade. Cut flowering heads and mature stalks down to ground-level growth. Lift every three years, plant out the most robust growth, and use the rest in compost. Gloves and long sleeves are needed when working with nettles. There is a less robust annual variety which makes its appearance in many gardens and may be used in the same way as the perennial variety.

ORIGANUM SPECIES (MARJORAM)

The most common varieties are:
Origanum majorana (knot marjoram, sweet marjoram)
O. onites (pot marjoram)
O. vulgare (oregano)

Sweet marjoram

Origin

Southeastern Europe and Asia Minor.

Culinary Uses

Oregano is aromatic and has a sweetly spicy flavour.

O. majorana
Because of its less robust, slightly sweet flavour, this variety enhances fish, eggs, salad, salad dressing, chicken, soups, stews, herb butters and cottage cheese. Add a sprig to a mixed herb tea. For flavouring cooked dishes, discard the stems, chop the leaves and stir in during the last few minutes of cooking.

Oregano

O. onites and *O. vulgare*
These varieties have a more robust flavour and a spicier fragrance than *O. majorana* and are best used in pizza and with pasta.

Medicinal Uses

Make a tea of 5 ml (1 tsp) chopped, dried or 15 ml (1 tbsp) fresh marjoram leaves to 250 ml (½ pt) boiling water to treat both insomnia and a nervous headache. This tea is also a comforting drink when you are suffering from a bad cold.

Pot marjoram

Origanum majorana

Height 30 cm (12 in). This variety has compact, bushy growth and thin stalks of soft, veined, grey/green, oblong leaves. The slender stems bear knot-like buds. The sweetly scented flowers are pinkish-white.

Origanum onites

It is low growing until the flowers appear. Dark green, heart-shaped leaves occur on purple-tinged, hairy stems. The flowers are mauve.

Origanum vulgare

Height 90 cm (35 in) when in flower. This variety has coarse, wiry stalks with slightly longer, greener leaves than those of *O. majorana*. The buds are looser and the flowers are white. Flower colours range from rose and purple to palest pink and white.

Other Uses

Marjoram is a pleasant bath herb. These varieties make attractive cut flowers and, when dried, add a spicy fragrance to potpourri. To dry, cut long stems before the flowers open, make a bunch and then use the bag method (see page 16).

Cultivation

This herb is a perennial. Seed can be sown in trays in spring or cuttings taken, but root division is generally the quickest way of propagating it. *O. majorana* also lends itself well to layering. Sun and a well-drained soil are required. It will grow in semi-shade but watch out for downy mildew. It is suitable for growing in containers. *O. majorana* is frost-sensitive. To keep plants neat, cut out all dead wood and remove dead flowers and stalks, making sure that there is still plenty of foliage on the bushes. *O. onites* should be cut down to new growth near the ground. There are many varieties, some with golden foliage like the creeping Golden Marjoram.

Pests and Diseases

Australian bug and downy mildew (see page 11).

PARSLEY

Petroselinum crispum
(curled parsley)
P. var. *neapolitanum*
(Italian parsley)

Origin

Sardinia, Turkey, Algeria.

Culinary Uses

This is a herb to enhance the flavour of most savoury cooking. Sprigs of curled parsley make a fresh, green

Curled parsley

Italian parsley

garnish. It is one of the herbs in *fines herbes* and *bouquet garni*. Parsley is usually finely chopped and added to food a few minutes before serving, or scattered over food. For a garnish with a difference, take sprigs of parsley, rinse and shake dry. Deep-fry until just crisp, drain on a paper towel and serve with any grilled or fried food. To dry parsley, rinse well to remove grit and sand, shake dry and spread on a muslin-covered rack; alternatively, dry on trays in a cool oven until crisp. It may also be finely chopped and frozen in ice cubes for future use in soups and stews.

Medicinal Uses

As parsley is so rich in vitamins, trace elements and minerals, it should certainly be included in the daily diet. It is taken as a tea to aid digestion, it is used as a diuretic and it has been found helpful as an anti-inflammatory. The suggested dosage is approximately 30 ml (2 tbsps) fresh parsley chopped each morning and added to savoury food (sandwiches, eggs, soups, salads) to be eaten during the day.

Petroselinum crispum

Height 25 cm (10 in). It has a taproot producing a number of ridged stalks. The foliage branching from the upper stalk is dark green, curled and crisp. The flowers are pretty, small and greenish-yellow in the form of umbels.

Petroselinum var. *neapolitanum*

Height 45 cm (18 in). It has a deep taproot from which a number of ridged stalks fan out. The dark green, tender foliage is smooth and the flat leaves are deeply serrated, similar to those of celery.

Other Uses

A parsley solution makes a good skin tonic. Store it in the fridge until needed. Chew parsley to sweeten the breath. Curled parsley makes a decorative border plant. Roses also benefit from an under-planting of this herb. In China it is known as 'kill flea' – maybe!

Cultivation

Parsley is a biennial. To ensure a constant supply, it is advisable to sow small quantities of seed throughout the year. Sow the seed in trays. To speed up the slow germination (three weeks), steep seed in lukewarm water overnight or place in the freezer for 24 hours. Warm the soil by pouring hot water over the tray *before* sowing seed. Do not allow trays to dry out. Transplant the seedlings while young (four- to six-leaf stage) as moving the more mature plants causes early bolting. Parsley requires a rich, moist soil in sun or semi-shade. Italian parsley may grow for four years before bolting, especially if the middle of the plant is snipped regularly. If parsley is left in the bed until the seeds are dry, it will self-sow readily. Curled parsley is most suitable for containers and hanging baskets.

Pests

Caterpillars (see page 11).

PELARGONIUMS (SCENTED)

Pelargonium graveolens (rose)
P. capitatum (rose)
P. citriodorum (lemon)
P. tomentosum (peppermint)

There are more than 50 listed scented pelargoniums so it is advisable to look for the different varieties at your local nurseries and also in the gardens of fellow herb growers.

Pelargoniums

Rose geranium (graveolens)

Lemon geranium

Pelargonium citriodorum

Height over 1 m (3 ft). This variety has stiff, upright, woody growth. The leaves are firm, light green and deeply toothed. The small flowers are a dark shade of pink. It has a strong lemon fragrance.

Rose geranium (capitatum)

Peppermint pelargonium

Pelargonium tomentosum

Origin

Southern Africa.

Culinary Uses

P. graveolens and *P. capitatum*
Flavour stewed apples, pears and apple jelly with whole leaves. For cakes and fruit tarts, line the tins with leaves. To get them to lie flat, dip in hot water and shake dry. For custards or milk puddings, steep the leaves in hot milk for 10 minutes, then remove. Chop finely before mixing into biscuit or scone dough. A leaf improves a mixed herb tea. Flowers may be used as a garnish.

P. citriodorum
As you would with rose geranium, flavour custards and milk puddings

This herb has a sprawling, loose growth. The leaves are rounded and slightly indented with a soft, velvety texture. These deep green leaves grow on longer stems than the other varieties. There are loose clusters of small white flowers with red lines on the upper petals. It has a strong peppermint fragrance.

Pelargonium capitatum

Height 80 cm (32 in). This variety is a woody subshrub with a compact growth. *P. capitatum* has shallow indentations on rounded leaves with wavy edges, and it has clusters of small pink flowers. (*P. graveolens* has deeply indented, light green, firm leaves.) The rose fragrance varies with growing conditions.

by steeping leaves in the hot milk for 10 minutes. Add leaves to a herb tea. Flowers are used as a garnish.

P. tomentosum
For a chocolate cake, line the bottom of the tin with leaves. Flavour stewed pears with leaves. Small flowers may be used as a garnish, particularly for chocolate desserts.

Other Uses

Pelargonium is a herb for a scented bath. Dry it for potpourri by spreading leaves on a rack to dry. (Peppermint pelargonium is a slow drier so remove the stems to speed up the process.) Add the leaves to a posy or small flower arrangement. A few leaves put into the vacuum cleaner bag will scent the house. When using a tumble drier, tie a few leaves in old, clean tights and place this among the clothes to scent them as they dry. Commercial oil is extracted from both *P. graveolens* and *P. capitatum*.

Cultivation

Propagate pelargoniums from cuttings, or if mature plants have sent out rooted suckers, carefully remove from the mother plant and then grow in bags of average soil until established. Pelargoniums can be grown from seed sown in trays. Grow in full sun in well-drained, average soil. Take care to water well during hot weather. Peppermint pelargonium does better when it is planted in the shade of a tree or shrub and allowed to grow up into the branches. This has the advantage of keeping soil off the leaves. Rose and lemon varieties are suitable for growing in a large container.

PINEAPPLE SAGE

Salvia elegans

Origin

Mexico.

Pineapple sage

Salvia elegans

Height 1 m (3 ft). It has upright, firm, reddish stems and soft, green leaves, the edges of which are tinged with red as they mature. From late summer into winter, there are delicate spikes of long, scarlet flowers.

Culinary Uses

The leaves and flowers have a taste and fragrance of pineapple. Whole flowers and snipped young leaves are used in fresh vegetable and fruit salads. Add mature leaves to a herbal tea. Chopped leaves are added to chicken and pork dishes at the end of the cooking time, or to any other food which is enhanced by a pineapple flavour.

Other Uses

It is a decorative plant providing winter colour. The flower spikes last in water when cut.

Cultivation

Pineapple sage is a perennial which spreads by suckers but is not so invasive as to become a problem.

Propagate by lifting and separating clumps or by semi-hard cuttings in spring. Grow in sun or semi-shade in well-composted, light soil. Cut back to base after flowering. Pineapple sage is frost-sensitive.

PURSLANE

Portulaca oleracea
(common purslane)
P. oleracea subsp. *sativa*
(cultivated purslane)

Origin

North Africa, Middle East and Asia.

Common purslane

Culinary Uses

It has a delicate 'green' flavour. Chop leaves and stems and add to soups and stews before serving; this will add to the nutritional value of the food. For salads, strip the leaves from the stems. Chop leaves lightly and mix them into a mayonnaise,

Portulaca oleracea

This herb has a low-growing, sprawling habit. It has succulent, reddish stems which bear smooth, succulent, rounded leaves. The dark green leaves have a thin, red edging. The flowers are small and yellow.

Portulaca oleracea subsp. *sativa*

Height 25 cm (10 in). The foliage of this variety is more succulent than common purslane and the flowers larger.

which is especially good with fish. Cook purslane as a vegetable in the minimum amount of water. Pickle stalks of leaves in spiced vinegar. Once the flowers appear, the quality of the plant deteriorates.

Cultivation

Purslane is an annual which self-sows. It is usually found growing like a weed. If no commercial seed is available, acquire a few young plants from a friend's garden for starters. Because of a long taproot, mature plants do not transplant well. They will survive under poor conditions, but for lush growth plant in rich soil and water well. They are suitable for container growing.

ROCKET

Eruca sativa

Origin

Southern Europe and Western Asia.

Rocket

Eruca sativa

Height 50 cm (20 in). It starts as a loose rosette of smooth, dark green, deeply indented leaves which grow to 20 cm (8 in) long. The purplish stems bear leaves which become smaller and slightly pointed towards the flowering tips The purple-tinged buds produce simple yellow and white flowers. The seed pods are about 5 cm (2 in) in length, turning a pale biscuit colour before opening, to scatter round, black seeds.

Culinary Uses

Rocket has a nutty, mustard flavour. It is an excellent herb for salads and sandwiches. Buds and flowers may be stirred into cottage cheese or used as a garnish. Leaves, flowers, buds and green seed pods are all used fresh.

Cultivation

Rocket is an annual sown in situ. As plants mature quickly, sow continuously throughout the year, except in areas of frost or intense heat. Grow in clumps so that the plants support each other – single plants tend to straggle. If transplanting seedlings, do so when four leaves appear. Transplantings tend to bolt early. Grow in a sunny position in well-composted soil. If commercial seed is not available, obtain a plant from a nursery or a friend and collect the seed. Sow some of it immediately. Established plants tend to self-sow.

ROSEMARY

Rosmarinus officinalis
(common rosemary)
R. officinalis var. (McConnell's Blue rosemary)
R. prostrata (trailing rosemary)
Eriocephalus africanus
(wild rosemary)

Origin

Mediterranean region and Asia minor. Wild rosemary – South Africa.

Culinary Uses

Rosemary is strongly aromatic with a resinous flavour. Chop leaves otherwise they fall off the stems during cooking and are unpleasant to chew. Chopped leaves may be used to flavour breads, scones and biscuits. Cook rosemary in stews and soups and scatter over vegetables. Use sparingly. When roasting meats or poultry, whole sprigs are used and removed before serving. Rosemary is a good agent for flavouring oils and vinegars (see page 17). The flowers are pretty and tasty in a salad, herb butter and cottage cheese and they make an attractive garnish.

McConnell's Blue rosemary

Common rosemary

Trailing rosemary

Wild rosemary

Medicinal Uses

For a quick pick-me-up, aid to digestion or to alleviate a headache, make a tea using a 5 cm (2 in) sprig in 250 ml (½ pt) boiling water. As an antiseptic to wash wounds, use three sprigs. For bruises, sprains, aching muscles and joints, purchase rosemary oil, or one blended with other herbs like arnica and lavender.

Other Uses

A rosemary bath revitalizes. As a hair rinse, pour 250 ml (½ pt) boiling water over 30 ml (2 tbsps) crushed leaves, allow to steep for 30 minutes and strain. Use as it is or mix fifty-fifty with shampoo and keep in the fridge until required. Dry it by bunching and hanging and add it to potpourri, or use on its own as an effective moth deterrent.

Cultivation

Propagate by sowing seed in a tray, or better still, by taking heel cuttings or by layering. Prepare the soil well before planting, as rosemary will grow in one position for up to 30 years. Dig a hole measuring 40 x 40 cm (16 x 16 in). Work in compost, well-rotted manure, a handful

Rosmarinus officinalis

Height 1–1.5 m (3–5 ft). It has a sturdy, bushy growth which becomes woody with maturity. The branches carry long, narrow, leathery leaves which are dark green with greying undersides. The leaf edges tend to curl under upon themselves. Pale blue flowers appear from midsummer onwards, clustered among the leaves towards the top of slender branches.

Rosmarinus officinalis var. 'McConnell's Blue'

Height 1 m (3 ft). It tends to grow into its own attractive shape, both upwards and sideways. Dark green, narrow leaves grow more densely than those of *R. officinalis*. The flowers are a deep, true blue.

Rosmarinus prostrata

This variety has a low-growing trailing habit. Firm, slender stems bear dense, dark green, narrow leaves. The flowers are a pale shade of blue.

Eriocephalus africanus

Height 1 m (3 ft). Its woody growth bears tender stems of close-growing, narrow, grey leaves with clusters of dainty, simple white flowers which in turn become fluffy grey balls. It is indigenous to Southern Africa.

of bone meal and another of hoof-and-horn. A sunny, well-drained position is required. Wild rosemary will grow in poor soil as it is a plant of the veld. Rosemary does not like wet roots. As its name, 'dew of the sea', implies, it is ideal to grow in seaside gardens. Hose down the foliage lightly during hot weather. Give it a good annual mulch of well-rotted manure. Common rosemary will make a hedge if kept pruned, otherwise just keep it in shape and remove dead wood. McConnell's Blue and trailing rosemary are best left unpruned as long as dead wood is removed. Trim wild rosemary to keep it in shape. *R. prostrata* is an excellent container plant and makes a magnificent show when trailed in a mass over walls and banks. There are other rosemary varieties with flowers ranging from white, pink and light blue to deep blue.

Pests

Australian bug (see page 11).

ROSES

Rosa

Origin

Persia (Iran), the East, Europe and Britain.

Culinary Uses

N.B. Do not use roses which have been sprayed with chemicals. The pale heel at the base of a rose petal is bitter, so remove it. Cut flowers when they are nearly open and, using the most fragrant petals, chop and mash into butter for sandwiches or for making cakes. Rose petals make a pretty and tasty sandwich filling and can also be scattered in a salad. Crystallize petals to use for decorating cakes, desserts and so on (see page 17). If there are enough deep red petals, make a few jars of jam (see page 17). Crush bright red and slightly soft rosehips before adding boiling water to make rose-hip tea. The coarse bud end of the hip must first be removed. Rosehips make excellent jam, and when cooked, puréed and sieved, they make a good base for various sauces. They are especially good with venison. Rose-water, which can be purchased from a pharmacy, can also be used in cooking.

Rose

Medicinal Uses

Rosehip syrup, high in vitamin C, is not practicable to make at home and may be purchased from a pharmacy or a health shop.

Other Uses

Rose-water is a most refreshing face tonic. Rose petals are an exotic and fragrant addition to your bath. Dry rose petals to use in potpourri. Always include some green leaves for colour. Use roses for hedges, arches and screens in the garden – they are both beautiful and practical.

Cultivation

Before planting a rose, prepare a hole measuring approximately 50 cm (20 in) square. The soil should be slightly acid. If necessary, add a handful of flowers of sulphur. A handful of bone meal should also be mixed in with compost and well-rotted manure. When planting out, make sure that the soil level in the hole is the same as it was in the bag. I usually slip the rose into the hole while still in the bag in order to check the levels. Remove the bag

Rosa

The flowers and foliage of the old varieties and the newer, highly fragrant species are too numerous and well-listed to warrant description here. Many original roses have been hybridized. While keeping their fragrance and form, they now produce two flowerings a year. Ask for Heritage roses at your local nursery or garden centre.

before you actually plant the rose. Roses grow equally well in sun or semi-shade, but in very hot areas Heritage roses need some protection from the harsh sun. Old-fashioned roses can be propagated either from cuttings or from hips. Roses grown from hips are interesting but not always true to form. Keep on deadheading unless hips are required. Prune lightly when the pruning time comes around. Roses make good container plants, providing the pot size is appropriate.

Pests and Diseases

The advantage of old-fashioned roses is that although they may become slightly diseased, they do not generally succumb to most rose ailments. Watch out for beetles and aphids (see page 11).

RUE

Ruta graveolens

Rue

Origin

Southern Europe and Middle East.

Ruta graveolens

Height 50 cm (20 in). Rue is a subshrub, branching close to the ground. The mature, slightly woody branches produce firm, grey/green stems of blue/grey leaves, giving the plant quite a lacy effect. Clusters of simple greenish-yellow flowers turn to attractive, green-lobed capsules of black seed. One variety, called Jackman's Blue, is a more compact, lower-growing plant with smaller, almost blue leaves.

Culinary Uses

This herb is bitter, pungent and highly aromatic and not commonly used in food. Some people add very small amounts to certain dishes and cordials. It is an ingredient of the Italian drink, grappa.

Medicinal Uses

Rue should only be taken under supervision as it has toxic properties. *N.B. Some skins are sensitive to this herb in hot weather. At the first signs of discomfort, and to avoid blistering, wash with soap and rinse well with cold water.*

Other Uses

Rue gives an attractive grey accent in the garden and is a long-lasting cut flower. A sprig in an arrangement prolongs the life of the other fresh flowers. Plant it under fruit trees to deter fruit fly. Rue lends itself to pruning to form a low hedge in, for example, a formal herb garden. A bunch hung at the kitchen window discourages flies. A small quantity in the dog's kennel or basket helps to keep fleas away. For dried arrangements, leave seed heads on plants until properly dry, then cut.

Cultivation

This herb is a perennial propagated by sowing seed in trays or by cuttings, root division or layering in spring. It self-sows freely. Transplant seedlings when 10 cm (4 in) high. Rue is not very fussy about position, but grows best in sun with average soil. Keep neat by cutting out old woody and seeded stems. Rue is frost-sensitive. If used as a hedge, keep well clipped. Jackman's Blue is suitable for growing in a container.

Pests

Caterpillars and snails (see page 11).

SAGE

Salvia officinalis

Origin

Spain and Mediterranean region.

Culinary Uses

Sage has a strong, warm and pungent flavour. For the best flavour, pick the younger leaves rather than the mature ones. Sage aids the

Sage

digestion of rich foods, therefore it is excellent cooked with oily fish and fatty meats and poultry. It is an important ingredient in certain pork sausages and it is a good herb to add to culinary oils and vinegars. The fresh, finely chopped leaves will add flavour to bread and scone doughs, or to cottage cheese. Use these sparingly for the best results. Sprinkle the chopped leaves over any cooked vegetables. The flowers are a decorative and tasty garnish. Cheddar cheese with sage is produced commercially. To freeze, chop and mix with a little water, then freeze in ice cubes.

Medicinal Uses

Chew a few sage leaves to alleviate a sore throat. To treat coughs and colds, make a tea of four or five leaves to 250 ml (½ pt) boiling water and flavour it with a little honey and lemon. An added sprig of thyme is effective. A slightly stronger brew makes a healing mouthwash for sore mouths. Sage acts as a tonic and is said to extend the life span.

Salvia officinalis

Height 35–60 cm (14–24 in). Sage is a subshrub with flexible stems. The leaves when young are oval and pale green, maturing to grey with a wrinkled, pebbled surface. The spikes of flowers are usually blueish-mauve or pink. There are varieties with white and deep blue flowers.

The following are some of the most common varieties of sage which are readily available:

Salvia officinalis var. *purpurea*
This variety has reddish-purple leaves and it seldom flowers.

Salvia officinalis var. *purpurea variegata*
The leaves are streaked with cream. It has blue flowers.

Salvia officinalis var. *tricolour*
It has purple, green and cream-streaked leaves.

Salvia aurea
The leaves are streaked with gold.

Other Uses

As a hair rinse, simmer 10 leaves with 500 ml (1 pt) water for about 10 minutes, cool and store for future use. To darken greying hair, add about 20 ml (4 tsps) of used tea leaves to the mixture. Strain before use. As sage is a natural deodorant, use it as a bath herb. Dried sage is added to potpourri for its anti-moth properties. Cut long stems before flowering to bunch, hang and dry.

Cultivation

Sage is a perennial with an average life span of four years. Sometimes, for no reason, a sage plant will curl up and die, so it is advisable to keep extra plants growing in bags. Grow this herb from seed sown in trays or by cuttings, root division or layering, done in spring and autumn. Full sun and a well-drained, light, slightly alkaline soil are required. Sage does not like wet roots. Cut back after flowering and remove dead wood. Protect the plants from cold, wind and frost. Sage is also suitable for container growing.

Pests and Diseases

Australian bug, grasshoppers and damp roots (see page 11).

SALAD BURNET

Sanguisorba minor subsp. *muricata* (=*Poterium sanguisorba*)

Origin

Mediterranean region and some parts of Asia Minor.

Culinary Uses

Salad burnet has a cucumber flavour. Fresh leaves (except those forming the centre crown) are stripped from stems and used whole in salads and sandwiches. Shred the

Salad Burnet

Sanguisorba minor subsp. *muricata*

Height 45 cm (18 in) in flower. It grows in the form of a rosette with stems falling outward. Slender stems bear many pairs of small, round, serrated leaves of a soft green to give a fern-like effect. Long, firm stems bear thimble-like, green heads of flowers from which reddish, thread-like pollen sacs hang.

leaves for herb butters and cottage cheese. Leafy stems are attractive and tasty as a garnish. Stems and leaves may be cooked in delicately flavoured cream soups, like mushroom, chicken and so on.

Other Uses

Steep leaves to make a skin tonic, and a handful of foliage makes a refreshing bath. Flower heads are decorative either fresh or dried. Burnet is an attractive foliage plant in the garden.

Cultivation

Salad burnet is a perennial. If no commercial seed is available, obtain a plant and propagate by root division. Burnet self-sows readily in situ. Do not allow too many flower heads to mature as there will be a surfeit of seedlings. Grow plants as a group or as a border. They do best in their own company. Burnet requires a sunny position with average soil. Keep well watered during hot weather. Remove dead leaves from the outer edge of the plant and unwanted flower stems as they appear. The herb is frost-sensitive. It is suitable for container growing.

Santolina

SANTOLINA

Santolina chamaecyparissus
S. neapolitana (cotton lavender)

Origin

Mediterranean coastal region.

Santolina

Uses

S. neapolitana has a sweetly pungent aroma. *S. chamaecyparissus* is sharply aromatic. Dried santolina is used in cupboards, drawers and bookcases to deter moths and silverfish. It is most effective. Scattered freshly in kennels and dog and cat baskets, it discourages fleas. It gives a decorative grey accent in a garden. *S. chamaecyparissus* lends itself to being clipped into a low, neat hedge, especially suitable for a formal herb garden. The flowers last well in fresh arrangements and may be cut at any time from the first show of colour to maturity. The foliage softens the appearance of a tussie mussie (see page 21). The flowers keep their colour when

Santolina chamaecyparissus

Height 45 cm (18 in). This variety is a subshrub with firm stems of close-growing, narrow, toothed, grey leaves – it looks a bit like coral. The flowers are exactly the same as those of *S. neapolitana*.

Santolina neapolitana

Height 60 cm (24 in). It is a subshrub tending to grow outwards. Loose stems of soft, grey leaves give the plant a feathery overall appearance. Long and slender stems bear golden yellow, button-like flowers with fluffy edgings.

dried. Dry the foliage and flowers to add to potpourri. Wait until the flowers are fully open before cutting for drying purposes and then bunch and hang to dry.

Cultivation

Santolina is a perennial, propagated from heel cuttings and layering in spring and autumn. A sunny position with average, well-drained soil is required. Give a mulch of compost and well-rotted manure annually. Prune back after flowering to prevent plants becoming too floppy or untidy. Santolina does well in coastal gardens, but it is frost-sensitive. *S. chamaecyparissus* is suitable for container planting. *S. neapolitana* may also be grown in a suitably large container.

Pests

Australian bug (see page 11).

SAVORY

Satureja montana (winter savory)
S. hortensis (summer savory)

Origin

Mediterranean region and Near East.

Culinary Uses

Savory has quite a strong, peppery flavour. The flavour of summer savory is the stronger of the two kinds. Cut the stems and strip as required. Chop finely and add to soups and stews towards the end of the cooking time. Rub it into meats and poultry before roasting or grilling. Scatter a small amount of chopped savory over a salad. Cook it with all types of beans, dried or green, and with other legumes. Savory makes a flavoursome oil and vinegar. To freeze, chop and mix with a little water, then pour it into ice cube compartments.

Winter savory

Medicinal Uses

Crush and apply savory to insect bites and stings. Make a digestive tea with one short sprig of winter savory or two of summer savory to 250 ml (½ pt) boiling water.

Summer savory

Satureja montana

Height 25 cm (10 in). It is a low-growing, compact plant. It is woody close to the ground with tender stems of leathery, dark green leaves, somewhat like rosemary in appearance. In late summer there are sprigs of small, pure white flowers.

Satureja hortensis

Height 35 cm (14 in). Slender, erect stems bear sparsely placed, pointed, bronze leaves. It has a softer growth than *S. montana*. The flowers are pale pink in colour.

Other Uses

Savory makes pretty cut flowers as well as foliage. To dry it, bunch together the stems and the foliage and hang upside down.

Cultivation

S. montana is perennial, propagated by tip and heel cuttings or layering. It requires well-drained, average soil in a sunny position. Cut back after flowering. It is frost-sensitive and suitable for growing in a container.

S. hortensis is an annual. Sow seed in trays or in situ throughout spring and summer. Germination is rapid, approximately 10 days. Grow fairly close for self-support. It requires a sunny position and rich soil.

Pests

Summer savory: Slugs and snails (see page 12).

SORREL

Rumex acetosa (French sorrel)
R. scutatus (Buckler sorrel)

Origin

Europe and North Africa.

Culinary Uses

Sorrel has a sharp, acid lemon flavour. The leaves of Buckler sorrel are very tender. Cut the leaves with the stems, wash, shake and roll in a tea towel. Keep in the fridge until required. Shred the leaves for sandwiches with meat or vegetable extract, cottage cheese or any other fillings. Tear the leaves for salad. Make an interesting cream soup from the leaves and stalks. Use sorrel to enhance a white sauce or add it to a butter sauce for fish. Cook it gently as for spinach. *N.B. People with inflammatory complaints of the joints and muscles should eat sorrel with discretion because of its high oxalic acid content.*

French sorrel

Medicinal Uses

Crush sorrel and use as an antidote for nettle stings and insect bites.

Cultivation

Sorrel is a perennial. Propagate it either by sowing seed in trays or by dividing clumps. *R. scutatus* is easily

Buckler sorrel

Rumex acetosa

Height 40 cm (16 in). It grows in thick clumps. Crisp, bright green, broad, oval leaves form an inverted 'V' to make them arrow-shaped at the base where they join smooth, brittle stems.

Rumex scutatus

It has a low-growing, spreading habit. The light green, shield-shaped leaves are blotched with silver. There is also a grey/green variety which is also blotched.

propagated by layering or dividing clumps. (Do not disturb too often.) *R. acetosa* should be lifted, divided and planted out every two or three years. For *R. acetosa*, dig the ground to a spade's depth, compost well and mix in a handful each of bone meal and hoof-and-horn. The roots of *R. scutatus* do not go down very deep. Grow sorrel in semi-shade to protect the tender leaves from sunburn. Occasionally apply a dressing of well-rotted manure, as these plants are greedy feeders. Water well in hot weather as the leaves tend to droop. Remove the flowering stems as they appear if the seed is not required. *R. acetosa* will grow in a deep container and *R. scutatus* in a fairly shallow one.

Pests

Slugs and snails (see page 12).

SOUTHERNWOOD

Artemisia abrotanum (Lad's Love or Maiden's Ruin)

Origin

Southern Europe and Middle East.

Southernwood

Artemisia abrotanum

Height 60 cm (24 in). Southernwood is a woody subshrub with sprigs of fine, feathery, dull grey/green leaves and insignificant flowers.

Uses

It has an aromatic, slightly bitter aroma. It is a potent anti-moth herb. The French call it 'garde-robe'. Dry it by bunching and hanging and add it to potpourri or use on its own. Southernwood is one of the herbs used in a lover's posy or tussie mussie. When southernwood is kept well clipped, it makes a suitable low hedge for a formal herb garden. It is said to prevent baldness and make young men's beards grow. There is no evidence to prove this.

Cultivation

Propagate it from semihardwood cuttings in spring and autumn. It requires a light, well-drained soil in full sun or semi-shade. Keep well pruned to prevent the plant looking leggy – there might be some dieback in winter. Remove flower heads as they appear. It is suitable for a large container if the plant is well shaped.

TANSY

Tanacetum vulgare (common tansy)
T. vulgare var. *crispum* (curly tansy)

Origin

Europe.

Common tansy

Tanacetum vulgare

Height when in flower 1 m (3 ft). This variety is low-growing with loose, deeply indented, green leaves on red-tinged stems. Firm, upright stems bear clusters of small, yellow, button-like flowers.

Tanacetum vulgare var. *crispum*

Height in flower 60 cm (24 in). The foliage is compact, crisp, fern-like and a bright lime green. When the flowers do appear, they are clusters of small yellow buttons.

Curly tansy

Cultivation

Tansy is a perennial. Propagate it by root division in spring and autumn. It has a spreading root habit which can prove quite invasive in a good locality. It requires full sun or semi-shade as well as an average, slightly alkaline soil. Tansy may die back in winter. Cut off all dead flowering stalks and remove all dead leaves, as slugs and snails tend to lurk around the plants. Tansy is frost-sensitive.

TARRAGON

Artemisia dracunculus

Origin

Southern and Central Europe.

Culinary Uses

This herb has a warm, aromatic taste. Good tarragon has a slight numbing after-effect on the tongue. It is one of the ingredients of *fines herbes*. Strip the tips and leaves from the mature stems. Finely chopped, fresh tarragon enhances the flavour of poultry, vegetables (especially

Uses

Tansy has an acrid, spicy fragrance. It is no longer used as a culinary herb as it has been found to have toxic properties. Hang bunches of fresh tansy in the kitchen to deter flies, and spread crushed leaves on shelves to stop ants. It is a decorative plant, especially the curly variety, although this seldom flowers. Dried tansy is a pleasant anti-moth herb and is also added to potpourri. To dry the flowers and foliage, cut, tie in bunches and hang up. Tansy is also an important compost activator.

Tarragon

green beans), eggs, mayonnaise, cream and butter sauces and salad dressings. Tarragon is an ideal herb to use for flavoured vinegars and oils. Use it sparingly in butters and cottage cheeses. To freeze, chop and add to a little water in an ice cube tray. Tarragon does not dry very well, so use it fresh and cut the stems approximately 15 cm (6 in) above the base of the plant.

Cultivation

Tarragon is a perennial. Propagate it from 15 cm (6 in) semihardwood cuttings in late spring, or by root division. Grow in a sheltered, sunny position in the ground or in a container. The soil must be rich and well drained, otherwise the roots will rot. Lift and divide it every two or three years. Tarragon dies back completely in winter so mark the place and protect the roots with a thick mulch. New shoots will appear in early spring. Tarragon is not the easiest herb to grow. Another variety, called *Artemisia dracunculoides* (Russian), grows much more freely but the flavour is slightly bitter and not very aromatic.

Artemisia dracunculus

Height 60 cm (24 in). It has a creeping, fibrous root system from which grow thin, wiry stalks. The long, glossy, narrow leaves have oil glands on the undersides. It is a dense, sprawling, bushy plant.

THYME

Thymus vulgaris (common thyme)
T. citriodorus (lemon thyme)

Origin

Mediterranean region.

Culinary Uses

Thyme has a strong, piquant and lemony flavour. For fresh use, cut throughout the year, though the flavour is best just before flowering. Strip small leaves from stems and use in any savoury dish. Thyme complements meat, fish and poultry. Chop and mix into dumplings, scones and breads. Blend a little into herb butter and cottage cheese. Add it to herb vinegars and oils. Thyme is also a *bouquet garni* herb.

Medicinal Uses

To soothe a cough, make a tea with a 10 cm (4 in) sprig of thyme and two sage leaves to 250 ml (½ pt) of boiling water. A stronger brew makes a healing mouthwash for sore gums and may be used as an antiseptic wash for wounds.

Common thyme

Other Uses

T. citriodorus makes a good ground cover. Dry for potpourri using the bag method (see page 16), as the small leaves tend to drop.

Cultivation

Thyme is a perennial. *T. vulgaris* is propagated from seed sown in a tray in spring, also by dividing mature plants, layering or cuttings made in spring and autumn. To propagate *T. citriodorus*, carefully remove the rooted sections from the side of the plant or sow seed. It requires full sun and a well-drained, light alkaline soil. Cut out all the old wood from

Thymus vulgaris

Height 30 cm (12 in). Common thyme is a subshrub with tough, woody branches from which grow more tender stems of small, stalkless, thin, dark grey/green leaves. In summer, the tips of the stems bear whorls of pale pink flowers.

Thymus citriodorus

Height 15 cm (6 in). Lemon thyme is a low-growing herb with soft, round, lemon-flavoured leaves. The flowers are a pinky-mauve. There is also a variegated form which makes an even prettier border plant.

Lemon thyme

T. vulgaris, remove the dead flower heads and neaten the plant. Cut back the dead flower heads from *T. citriodorus*. Thyme is suitable for container planting. It is sensitive to frost. There are many varieties of thyme, varying in height, foliage and colouring, with flowers shading from white to the deepest purple.

Pests

Australian bug (see page 11).

VIOLET

Viola odorata (sweet violet)

Origin

Europe and Britain.

Culinary Uses

Crystallize the fragrant flowers (see page 17) or else use them fresh to decorate cakes and desserts. Scatter flowers in summer beverages as well

Violet

as in salads. To make bland, pale soups look more interesting and colourful, stir in a few flowers.

Medicinal Uses

To make a violet tea, add about five leaves and four flowers to 250 ml (½ pt) boiling water. Drink this tea as a calmative and mild laxative. It will also relieve a tension headache.

Other Uses

It makes a pretty ground cover or edging plant. For potpourri, dry the flowers face down on a rack.

Cultivation

Violet is a perennial. Propagate it with leafy root crowns taken from runners. Plant firmly in soil, leaving a portion of crown above the ground. Lift and divide every second year after the flowering period. Violets require a rich, moist, slightly acid soil and will grow in semi-shade or sun. Shelter them from the midday sun in hot areas. If growing in shade, remove some of the foliage to increase flowering. Violets are suitable for container planting.

Viola odorata

Height 10–15 cm (4–6 in). Rhizomes with tough, hairy roots produce rooting runners. Slender, firm stalks bear dark green, glossy, heart-shaped leaves. The stems are curved at the flowering heads. The flowers are five-petalled with short, fleshy spurs. There are also double varieties. The flowers are usually deep purple. Other colours range from white to pink and soft blue.

WORMWOOD

Artemisia absinthium

Origin

Temperate areas of Europe and Asia.

Culinary Uses

The volatile oils having a very bitter taste and aroma, some cooks use just a trace of this herb in fatty meat dishes to aid digestion. At one time

Wormwood

wormwood was used to flavour absinthe, vermouth and tonic water. This practice was made illegal when it was found that this herb, if taken often, will affect both the nervous system and the eyesight.

Medicinal Uses

This herb is used in many pharmaceutical preparations. **N.B. Do not treat internal complaints with wormwood in its natural state.**

Other Uses

Dry the foliage and use it in antimoth bags for the storage of clothes. The dry leaves, sprinkled wherever ants are a problem, act as a deterrent. Grow wormwood under fruit trees in order to discourage codling moth. Make an anti-caterpillar spray from the foliage by simmering about 225 g (8 oz) wormwood leaves in 2 litres (4 pt) water for half an hour. Stir well, strain and allow to cool. Dissolve approximately 5 ml (1 tsp) soapflakes or dishwashing liquid in 500 ml (1 pt) hot water. Combine this liquid with the wormwood water and spray frequently at the height of the caterpillar season.

Artemisia absinthium

Height 60 cm (2 ft). It is a perennial with branched, leafy, ridged stems growing from a woody base. The deeply indented leaves are covered in fine hairs. They are grey green with silver undersides and they are approximately 10 cm (3 in) long.

Cultivation

It is an undemanding plant. It does best in a sunny position with good drainage and light soil. Propagate by root division or from semihardwood cuttings taken in autumn or spring.

YARROW

Achillea millefolium (woundwort or milfoil)

Origin

Caucasus and China.

Medicinal Uses

To staunch bleeding, crush yarrow leaves and press them against the wound for as long as is required.

Yarrow

Yarrow

Yarrow is a healing herb when it is used in the form of a poultice. To alleviate feverish cold symptoms, make a brew of a handful of yarrow leaves to 500 ml (1 pt) boiling water. Cool this, strain it and drink 125 ml (4 fl oz) twice a day. Honey and lemon will improve the taste.

Other Uses

Use fresh foliage for a soothing bath. Yarrow has a pungent, bitter-sweet fragrance. It is a colourful garden flower which cuts and dries well. Cut the stems of flowers at the base of the plant when at their height of colour, before the sun bleaches them. Bunch loosely and hang to dry. Yarrow flowers are a pretty, fragrant addition to potpourri. For the compost heap, dig out and use the surplus plants. This also helps to curb the root spread.

Cultivation

It is a perennial with a spreading, matted root system which needs to be controlled. Propagate by sowing in trays or by root division in spring. It requires sun and a light, well-drained soil. It will tolerate some shade and also fairly dry conditions. Replant every two or three years to prevent heavy matting which gives rise to fewer flowers. After flowering, cut back to base growth.

Disease

Mildew (see page 11).

Achillea millefolium

Height 30–60 cm (12–24 in), depending on the variety. Yarrow has ground-hugging, dull green, deeply cut, fern-like leaves. A long, firm, sparsely-leaved stem bears umbels of small, white flowers. Other varieties have flowers ranging from shades of yellow, pink, red, rose and apricot with variations in foliage from fern-like to feathery.

Yarrow

A variety of colourful herbs

MEDICINAL CHART

	Antiseptic	Bedwetting	Bleeding	Bruises & strains	Calmative	Chapped lips & blisters	Colds & influenza	Coughs & lung congestion	Digestive	Diuretic	Eyes	Hay fever	Headaches	Healing	Insomnia	Laxative	Mouthwash & ulcers	Rheumatism & related problems	Sore throat	Stings & insect bites	Tonic	Warts
Angelica					✽		✽		✽													
Basil																	✽					
Bay														✽								
Bergamot									✽										✽			
Borage								✽													✽	
Bulbine					✽									✽							✽	
Calendula			✽											✽								
Catnip		✽		✽																		
Celery										✽							✽					
Chamomile					✽		✽							✽	✽							
Chervil				✽					✽												✽	
Chickweed	✽									✽											✽	
Chives																						
Comfrey				✽										✽				✽			✽	
Coriander																						
Cress																						
Curry bush																						
Dandelion																					✽	✽
Dill									✽	✽												
Elder							✽	✽								✽						
Fennel				✽					✽		✽										✽	
Horehound							✽	✽											✽			
Horseradish									✽												✽	
Lavender	✽			✽	✽								✽		✽				✽			
Lemon balm					✽		✽						✽								✽	
Lemon grass																						
Lemon verbena					✽				✽													
Lovage									✽	✽												
Marjoram							✽						✽		✽							
Mint								✽	✽													
Nasturtium																				✽		
Nettle											✽											

CULINARY CHART

	Antiseptic	Bedwetting	Bleeding	Bruises & strains	Calmative	Chapped lips & blisters	Colds & influenza	Coughs & lung congestion	Digestive	Diuretic	Eyes	Hay fever	Headaches	Healing	Insomnia	Laxative	Mouthwash & ulcers	Rheumatism & related problems	Sore throat	Stings & insect bites	Tonic	Warts
Origanum																						
Parsley										✽												
Pelargonium, rose																						
Pelargonium, lemon																						
Pelargonium, peppermint																						
Pineapple sage																						
Purslane																						
Rocket																						
Rose																						
Rosemary	✽			✽					✽				✽				✽				✽	
Sage	✽						✽	✽	✽								✽		✽		✽	
Salad burnet																						
Savory									✽											✽		
Sorrel																				✽		
Tarragon																						
Thyme	✽							✽									✽					
Violet													✽									
Yarrow				✽				✽						✽								

GLOSSARY

Annuals
Plants grown from seed and never lasting more than a year.

Bi-annual
Flowering twice a year.

Biennial
Flowering in the second year.

Blanching
The covering of the lower parts of plants with soil or cloches to exclude light. This whitens and improves the flavour and texture.

Bolting
The rapid growth of a centre stem, ending in flowers and later seeds.

Boss
A knob-like protuberance.

Cloche
A covering of cardboard, opaque glass or other suitable material to exclude light from shoots or extended roots of plants.

Dead-heading
Removing dead flowers with a length of stem before seeding starts.

Harden off
To expose to sunlight by stages.

Heritage roses
Old-fashioned roses which have been hybridized to increase flowering time while retaining the disease-resistant qualities.

In situ
The position where seed is sown and plants are to grow. A method used for plants that do not transplant well.

Mulch
A layer of decomposed organic matter used to protect roots of plants.

Node
The joint on a stem from which a leaf grows.

Perennial
Living for many years.

Rose
An attachment placed on the end of the spout of a watering can to produce a fine spray.

Semi-hard cutting
Taken when new growth has begun to harden.

Soil
Acid soil has a reading below 6.0 on the pH scale. To create acid soil, dig in a good handful of flowers of sulphur or plenty of pine needles or oak leaves twice a year and when planting new plants.

Alkaline soil has a reading above 7.0 on the pH scale. To increase alkalinity, work in a little agricultural lime (dolomite).
Testing the pH level of soil is easy. If you own a swimming pool, take a little soil and use the pool testing equipment.

Stolon
An elongated shoot, producing roots from which a new plant is formed.

Suckers
Shoots from roots near the surface of the ground.

Umbels
Flat, round heads of small flowers.

INDEX

Achillea millefolium 74
Allium schoenoprasum 34
Allium tuberosum 34
Aloysia triphylla 48
Anethum graveolens 40
angelica 23
Angelica archangelica 23
Anthemis nobilis 31
Anthriscus cerefolium 32
ants 11
aphids 11
Apium graveolens 30
Armoracia rusticana 44
Artemisia abrotanum 70
Artemisia absinthium 74
Artemisia dracunculus 71
Australian bug 11

Barbarea verna 37
basil 24
    bush basil 24
    lettuce basil 24
    purple basil 24
    sweet basil 24
bath vinegars and oils 19
bay 25
bergamot 26
borage 27
Borago officinalis 27
bouquet garni 16
bulbine 28
Bulbine frutescens 28

calendula 28
calendula cream 19
Calendula officinalis 28
capers 16
caterpillars 11
catmint 29
catnip 30
celery 30
chamomile 31
    German chamomile 31
    Roman chamomile 31
chervil 32
chickweed 34
chives 34
    common chives 34
    garlic chives 34
comfrey 35
comfrey cream 19
comfrey foliar feed 14
companion planting 13
compost 8
containers 9
coriander 36
Coriandrum sativum 36
cosmetic uses 19
cottage cheese 16
creams 20
cress 37
    American cress 37
    garden cress 37
    watercress 38
crystallizing 17
culinary uses 16

curry bush 38
cuttings 10
Cymbopogon citratus 48

dandelion 39
dill 40

elder 40
Eriocephalus africanus 62
Eruca sativa 61

face tonics 20
facial steam 20
fennel 41
    bronze fennel 41
    common fennel 41
    Florentine fennel 41
feverfew 42
fines herbes 17
Foeniculum purpurascens 41
Foeniculum vulgare 41
Foeniculum vulgare var. *dulce* 41
fragrant uses 20
fungal diseases 11

general insect spray 14

hair rinses 20
Helichrysum petiolare 38
herb butters 16
herbal bath 19
herbal tea 19
home brews 14
horehound 43
horehound cough sweets 19
horseradish 44

Jeyes fluid spray 14

Lactuca sativa 49
Laurus nobilis 25
Lavandula angustifolia 44
Lavandula dentata 44
Lavandula dentata var. *candicans* 44
lavender 44
    English lavender 44
    French lavender 44
layering 10
lemon balm 46
lemon grass 48
lemon verbena 48
Lepidium sativum 37
lettuce 49
Levisticum officinale 50
lovage 50

marigold 52
    African marigold 52
    French marigold 52
    Inca marigold 52
Marrubium vulgare 43
Matricaria recutita 31
medicinal uses 17
Melissa officinalis 46
Mentha piperata 52
Mentha pulegium 52
Mentha rotundifolia 52
Mentha spicata 52

Mentha suaveolens 52
mint 52
    apple mint 52
    crinkle-leaved spearmint 52
    mint sauce 17
    pennyroyal 52
    peppermint 52
    spearmint 52
Monarda didyma 26

nasturtium 54
Nasturtium officinale 38
Nepeta cataria 30
Nepeta faassenii 29
nettle 55

Ocimum basilicum 24
Ocimum basilicum purpurascens 24
Ocimum crispum 24
Ocimum minimum 24
origanum species 56
    oregano 56
    pot marjoram 56
    sweet marjoram 56
Origanum majorana 56
Origanum onites 56
Origanum vulgare 56

parsley 57
    curled parsley 57
    Italian parsley 57
Pelargonium capitatum 58
Pelargonium citriodorum 58
Pelargonium graveolens 58
Pelargonium tomentosum 58
pelargoniums 58
    peppermint pelargonium 58
    lemon geranium 58
    rose geranium 58
pesto 17
pests and diseases 11
Petroselinum crispum 57
Petroselinum var. *neapolitanum* 57
pineapple sage 60
pistou 17
Portulaca oleracea 61
Portulaca oleracea subsp. *sativa* 61
potpourri 20
poultices 19
propagation and planting 9
purslane 61
    common purslane 61
    cultivated purslane 61

raised bed 9
ravigoti 17
red pepper spray 14
red spider 12
rocket 61
root division 10
Rosa 64
rose jam 17
rosemary 62
    common rosemary 62
    McConnell's Blue rosemary 62
    trailing rosemary 62
    wild rosemary 62
roses 64
Rosmarinus officinalis 62

Rosmarinus officinalis var. 'McConnell's Blue' 62
Rosmarinus prostrata 62
rue 65
Rumex acetosa 69
Rumex scutatus 69
rust 12
Ruta graveolens 65

sage 65
salad burnet 66
Salvia elegans 60
Salvia officinalis 65
Sambucus nigra 40
Sanguisorba minor subsp. *muricata* 66
santolina 67
    cotton lavender 67
Santolina chamaecyparissus 67
Santolina neapolitana 67
Satureja hortensis 68
Satureja montana 68
savory 68
    summer savory 68
    winter savory 68
scale 12
seed 9
    sowing in situ 10
    sowing in trays 9
slugs and snails 12
soil and site preparation 6
sorrel 69
    Buckler sorrel 69
    French sorrel 69
southernwood 70
Stellaria media 34
stink bugs 12
suckers 11
Symphytum officinale 35

Tagetes erecta 52
Tagetes minuta 52
Tagetes patula 52
Tanacetum parthenium 42
Tanacetum vulgare 71
Tanacetum vulgare var. *crispum* 71
tansy 71
    common tansy 71
    curly tansy 71
Taraxacum officinale 39
tarragon 71
thyme 72
    common thyme 72
    lemon thyme 72
Thymus citriodorus 72
Thymus vulgaris 72
tisane 19
Tropaeolum majus 54
tussie mussie 21

Urtica dioica 55

vinegars and oils 17
Viola odorata 73
violet 73

wormwood 74

yarrow 74